THE COMFORT FOOD MASH-UP COOKBOOK

ALSO BY DAN WHALEN

Stuffed
The Ultimate Comfort Food Cookbook

Tots!
50 Tot-ally Awesome Recipes from
Totchos to Sweet Po-tot-o Pie

THE COMFORT FOOD MASH-UP COOKBOOK

80 DELICIOUS RECIPES FOR REIMAGINING YOUR FAVORITE DISHES

DAN WHALEN

PHOTOGRAPHY BY
BRIAN SAMUELS

STERLING EPICURE
New York

STERLING EPICURE
New York

An Imprint of Sterling Publishing Co., Inc.
1166 Avenue of the Americas
New York, NY 10036

ISBN 978-1-4549-2325-1

Distributed in Canada by Sterling Publishing Co., Inc.
c/o Canadian Manda Group, 664 Annette Street
Toronto, Ontario M6S 2C8, Canada
Distributed in the United Kingdom by GMC Distribution Services
Castle Place, 166 High Street, Lewes, East Sussex BN7 1XU, United Kingdom
Distributed in Australia by NewSouth Books
45 Beach Street, Coogee, NSW 2034, Australia

For information about custom editions, special sales, and premium
and corporate purchases, please contact Sterling Special Sales at
800-805-5489 or specialsales@sterlingpublishing.com.

Manufactured in China

2 4 6 8 10 9 7 5 3 1

sterlingpublishing.com

Interior design by Aaron Taylor-Waldman
Food styling by Krissy Price

CONTENTS

INTRODUCTION

I cook a lot of different recipes on my website, The Food in My Beard, but, when I combine two classic foods into one unique dish, the Internet goes wild. Something about a new twist on iconic meals sparks a social media frenzy. I never set out to become the master of the mash-up, but, like Andy Warhol or the Beastie Boys before me, I have an eye for creative combination. At the beginning of my blogging efforts, I was mashing up recipes, although I never called it that back then. As I improved, it became my calling in the food world. Now, more than ten years later, I have become the go-to guy when the media wants to know more about mash-ups.

Mash-up recipes are fun. The appeal stems from taking nostalgic dishes and updating them with a modern twist. I love connecting with people in this way, and that's why mash-up recipes have become my favorite to create. I'm extremely excited to round up my favorite recipes, plus a bunch of awesome new ones, into this new cookbook for you.

I break down the source recipes, piece by piece. I think about each ingredient and what's essential to the final dish. How many ingredients can I remove but still call it by its name? I break down both dishes this way and then build them back up together. This makes the final product a true combination of both dishes, with no excess or unnecessary ingredients. When I wanted to make Fast-Food Burger Stuffing, instead of chopping up a couple of hamburgers and mixing them with stock and eggs, I looked at the flavors and ingredients of a classic fast-food burger and created a stuffing recipe from scratch that employed these flavors.

I follow and respect other bloggers who make mash-ups, but many of those over-the-top recipes end up full of processed food. They're bold, loud, and aim for the shock factor. Shock-blogger recipes aren't something that a family could eat even as an indulgent Sunday supper. They're more like 5,000-calorie bombs—more novelty than substance. My mash-ups are made almost entirely from scratch, and I want people to cook them. So these recipes aren't any more challenging than making dinner or more technical than their source recipes. Most aren't healthy by any means, but they won't give you instant diabetes either. Just as home cooks can make easy dishes inspired by elaborate tasting menus prepared with tweezers and a sous vide machine, my recipes take inspiration from some of these crazier concoctions, but they're completely approachable. Recipes generally appear from lighter to heavier order. Similar dishes cluster together, and adjacent recipes often feature overlapping ingredients.

A BRIEF HISTORY OF MASH-UPS

Mash-ups are having a moment—in art, movies, music, and TV. Food is no different. People regularly line up for Dominique Ansel's Cronuts® in New York City and for Korean tacos in Los Angeles like the launch of limited edition sneakers or their favorite band's farewell tour.

This trend might seem new, but it's been going on since the Mongol Empire brought noodles from Asia to Europe in the thirteenth century. The following iconic dishes have defined the mash-up trend over time.

1400s	**LAMB VINDALOO**	After Chicken Tikka Masala, Vindaloo is one of the most well-known Indian curry dishes, and both are more mash-up than authentic Indian. When the Portuguese colonized India, they brought with them a spicy meat stew made with wine and garlic (*de vinho de alho*). In Goa, a Portuguese colony in southwest India, the recipe gained curry spices, chile peppers, and potatoes because the Hindi word for potato, *aaloo*, sounds similar to *alho*, the Portuguese word for garlic.
1600s	**JAMAICAN PATTY**	The Cornish pasty came to Jamaica during colonial settlement, and the Jamaicans added cumin, curry, and scotch bonnet to the meat filling to make it their own. Jamaicans use a lot of curry in their food because many indentured servants came to the island from India.
1800s	**FISH & CHIPS**	This British staple blends techniques brought to London from all over Europe. Spanish Jews pioneered the breading and frying of fish, and frying potatoes into what we call French fries came from Belgium.
1900	**SPAGHETTI & MEATBALLS**	Noodles came from China to Europe in the 1200s, and the Spanish first encountered tomato plants in the New World in the 1500s. Italians eat meatballs not with the pasta but as a second course. At the turn of the twentieth century, Italian Americans combined these two separate courses into one (that I ate once a week thinking I was the most Italian kid on the block), so this dish contains a meta-blend of regions and cultures.

| 1910 | RAMEN | The history of ramen is as cloudy as the broth itself. The noodles are Chinese, and the broth is most likely Korean, but everyone knows that ramen is Japanese. |

| 1950 | BANH MI | When the French colonized Vietnam, they brought baguettes, mayonnaise, and pâté with them. When they left, the Vietnamese added hot sauce and cilantro and swapped the cornichons for pickled carrots and radish. |

| 1960 | BURRITOS | This quintessentially "Mexican" dish sprang to life in the Mission district of San Francisco. Traditional Mexican burritos or burros are smaller and often filled only with refried beans—what Americans would call a taquito. |

| 1970 | CALIFORNIA ROLL | One of the most famous types of sushi in America, this creation rolled into being in Vancouver, Canada, to help reluctant Westerners taste sushi for the first time without having to eat raw fish. |

| 1982 | SMOKED SALMON PIZZA | Wolfgang Puck often receives credit for being the father of fusion cuisine, even though it has existed since cooking began. When fusion trended hard in the 1990s, Puck was leading the charge. Many of his dishes from Spago, including Buffalo Chicken Spring Rolls, Barbecue Nachos, and this one, now appear on the menus of chain restaurants across the country. Ultimately, fusion became so popular then that an inevitable backlash occurred, and the word still has a negative connotation today. That's why we make mash-ups now instead of fusion dishes. Same thing, new name. |

| 2008 | KOREAN TACOS | Koji, the Korean-Mexican street food truck in Los Angeles, made mash-ups cool again. It wasn't a stuffy restaurant throwing together two watered-down Asian dishes and calling it fusion. It was a hip new eatery creating smart food combos that looked bright, tasted flavorful, and didn't cost a lot. |

| 2013 | CRONUT® | Dominique Ansel caused a stir and elevated the mash-up of breakfast and dessert by creating this hybrid of a donut and croissant at his Manhattan bakery. People lined up for *hours* to buy one. |

| 2013 | RAMEN BURGER | After the Cronut craze, many uninspired ripoffs—bonut, crogel, crognet, dough-sant, scronut—emerged to cash in on the public's newfound love of pastry mash-ups. Cutting through this fog of mediocrity came this burger patty served on a bun of congealed noodles. Its flavors came from Asia and America, and it helped cement mash-up cuisine in contemporary food culture. |

THE BLUEPRINT

There's no one formula for making mash-up recipes, but following a pattern makes it easier to create them. Generally speaking, there are two different types of mash-ups. The first integrates two dishes into one. With this method, the flavors of the two dishes meld, and certain bites taste slightly more like one or the other of the source dishes. This is the traditional mash-up.

For what I call the *smash-in*, you take the ingredients of one dish and convert it to the format of another dish. With this method, you want the flavors of one dish but the presentation of another, so think of a burger, burrito, or taco inspired by another dish.

Let's take a closer look at each method with some examples.

STEP 1

Define the ingredients needed for each separate dish.

 **MAC AND CHEESE**

INGREDIENTS

pasta

cheese

milk

breadcrumbs

 EVERYTHING BAGEL

INGREDIENTS

cream cheese

everything spice

bagel

Pair each list down to the essentials while looking for common ingredients.

Milk, cheese, and cream cheese are all pretty similar ingredients. The bagel can sub for the breadcrumbs, and the everything spice can flavor the sauce.

WHAT ARE
THE COMMON
INGREDIENTS?

STEP 3

Build it back up.

Sometimes I make a roux for mac and cheese, but a soft cheese can form the sauce on its own. For this recipe, the cream cheese acts as the base of the sauce, and the toasted bagel becomes the breadcrumb topping.

MAC AND CHEESE		EVERYTHING BAGEL MAC & CHEESE		EVERYTHING BAGEL
pasta	→	pasta		
cheese ß	→	cream cheese or cheese sauce	←	cream cheese
milk		everything spice	←	everything spice
breadcrumbs	→	toasted bagel pieces	←	bagel

STEP 4

Make and enjoy!

Cooking should be fun. If you've come this far, you really can't fail. Pay attention and taste as you go. Trust yourself, and you'll end up with something delicious.

Now let's look at the smash-in method with Lasagna Tacos as our example.

As before, define the necessary elements in each source dish.

LASAGNA

INGREDIENTS

pasta

beef or sausage

tomato sauce

ricotta

mozarella

basil

TACO

INGREDIENTS

tortilla shell

meat

salsa

sour cream

cheese

lettuce

Look for ingredients in the first source recipe that can work in place of ingredients in the second dish, either visually or structurally.

If you fry the pasta, for example, it can replace the taco shell. Replacing taco meat with sausage is pretty easy, but we have two cheeses in the lasagna and only one in the taco. The key here is the types of cheese. Use mozzarella to replace the taco cheese and ricotta to replace the sour cream. Tomato sauce easily replaces the salsa, and a sprinkle of basil replaces the lettuce.

LASAGNA		TACO
pasta	➝	tortilla shell
beef or sausage	➝	meat
tomato sauce	➝	salsa
ricotta	➝	sour cream
mozarella	➝	cheese
basil	➝	lettuce

Make and enjoy!

Again, remember to have fun with it and let your creativity run wild. See the Combo Charts on pages 180–187 to help you create your own crazy mash-ups and smash-ins!

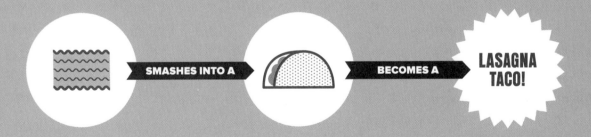

SMASHES INTO A   BECOMES A   LASAGNA TACO!

APPS & SNACKS

MAC & CHEESE DEVILED EGGS

MAKES	PREP TIME	COOK TIME	TOTAL TIME
16 deviled eggs	45 minutes	15 minutes	75 minutes

When I first thought about this one, I couldn't believe no one had done it before. It's sort of a no-brainer not only because the flavors work so well together but also because both dishes are so hot right now. Make this fun showstopper for the next party you attend or throw.

LEFTOVERS➡ This recipe makes a bit more pasta than you need, but the ratio works with the number of egg yolks, so the amount makes sense. Plus, the pasta is tasty on its own as leftovers.

8 jumbo eggs

8 ounces macaroni

⅔ cup milk

3 tablespoons butter

12 ounces cheddar cheese, shredded

4 slices bacon

2 teaspoons mustard

¼ cup chopped chives, plus extra for garnish

1 teaspoon paprika, plus extra for garnish

1. Hardboil the eggs and cool in an ice-water bath.

2. While the eggs are boiling, boil the pasta in salted water until the texture is al dente. Reserve ½ cup pasta water and strain.

3. Add the pasta back to the pot and add the milk, butter, and a splash of the pasta water. Bring to a simmer.

4. Stir in the cheese a few ounces at a time. Remove from heat and stir until the cheese fully melts and a thick sauce forms on the pasta. If it looks too thick, add another splash of pasta water, but remember that the sauce will thicken as it cools.

5. Cook the bacon until crisp. Cut into bite-size pieces.

6. Peel the eggs and cut in halves. Remove the yolks and crumble them into the pasta.

7. Stir the mustard, chives, and paprika into the pasta. If it looks too dry, heat it lightly again.

8. Spoon the pasta into the egg cavities, mounding it up so it looks heaping.

9. Top with a small piece of bacon and garnish with more chives and paprika to taste.

KIELBASA SUMMER ROLLS

MAKES	PREP TIME	COOK TIME	TOTAL TIME
15 rolls	4 hours 30 minutes	10 minutes	4 hours 30 minutes

You might look at this dish and wonder what the mash-up is, thinking, *He put kielbasa in a spring roll—big deal*. But it's a little more complex than that. One of my favorite appetizers is grilled or sauteed kielbasa dipped in a little mustard. I took that idea and integrated the flavors into a Vietnamese summer roll. This mash-up also represents another mash-up, the marriage of my close friends John, who is Polish, and Fiona, who is Vietnamese. I originally created this dish for their wedding shower.

DOUBLE BAG IT➡ You can find rice paper at most grocery stores these days. Some brands are thin, and others are thick, so, depending on what you get, they might need more time in the water bath or to be double wrapped.

1. In a glass measuring cup, microwave the vinegar on high for 2 minutes. Place the julienned carrots in a Mason jar or other sealable container along with the garlic and sugar. Season with salt and pepper to taste. Pour the hot vinegar over the carrots and add water if needed to fill the container and submerge the veggies. Set aside for at least 4 hours but preferably overnight.

2. Mix the sauce ingredients and allow to chill in the fridge while you make the rolls.

3. Strain and dry the carrots.

4. Sauté the kielbasa on medium-high heat for about 5 minutes per side to brown it lightly.

5. Into a shallow container bigger than the rice paper, such as a baking dish or frying pan, pour about 1 quart of water.

6. Dip a sheet of rice paper into the water for about 3 seconds. It might feel like it needs more time, but it will continue to soften.

7. Place the rice paper onto a clean, dry surface and place 2 basil leaves on it. Top with lettuce, carrots, and 2 rounds of kielbasa.

8. Roll it tightly by folding the paper over the filling, folding the sides in, and continuing to roll it up, as you would with a burrito.

9. Cut each roll in half and serve with the dipping sauce.

QUICK-PICKLED CARROTS

1 cup rice vinegar

5 large carrots, peeled and julienned

1 clove garlic

1 pinch sugar

salt and pepper

SAUCE

¼ cup mustard

2 tablespoons fish sauce

2 tablespoons Sriracha

1 tablespoon honey

1 tablespoon soy sauce

ROLLS

1 pound kielbasa, sliced into rounds

15 summer roll rice paper wrappers (more if doubling or if some break)

30 basil leaves

1 head iceberg lettuce, shredded

BLOODY MARY CEVICHE

MAKES	PREP TIME	COOK TIME	TOTAL TIME
4 servings	45 minutes	—	45 minutes

At the end of a bowl of ceviche, you usually have a little leftover liquid with a milky consistency and intense flavor. A Peruvian friend calls this *leche de tigre*, milk of the tiger. Whenever we ate ceviche together, at the end of the meal we mixed it with a little vodka and took a shot. I love this tradition and took the concept further by combining the cold, refreshing fish dish with my favorite savory cocktail. These dishes come together easily and even have a little shrimp cocktail flavor in the mix.

RAW & UNCUT

- This dish works with different types of fish, but shrimp is best because the tomato and horseradish evoke shrimp cocktail.
- Buy really good, fresh medium-size shrimp, around 41 to 50 pieces per pound.
- If you feel uncomfortable eating raw shrimp, sauté them for 3 minutes per side to cook them lightly instead of marinating them in the lime mixture. Still add the lemon and lime juices in step 3.

---

1. Mix the shrimp with the lemon and lime juices and season with salt and pepper to taste.

2. Stir in the garlic and shallot. Refrigerate for 30 minutes.

3. Mix the tomato juice, pickle juice, horseradish, Worcestershire sauce, hot sauce, vodka, and cilantro into the shrimp and stir to combine.

4. Divide into 4 glasses and serve with tortilla chips and the garnishes of your choice.

20 medium shrimp, cleaned and deveined, shells and tails removed

juice of 1 lemon

juice of 5 limes (about ½ cup)

salt and pepper

1 clove garlic, grated

1 shallot, minced

3 cups tomato juice

2 tablespoons pickle juice

1 tablespoon prepared horseradish

1 tablespoon Worcestershire sauce

2 teaspoons hot sauce

2 ounces vodka

¼ cup chopped cilantro

tortilla chips

celery, gherkins, olives, pickled carrots, or pickled jalapeño peppers for garnish

SUSHI ARANCINI

MAKES	PREP TIME	COOK TIME	TOTAL TIME
12 sushi balls	25 minutes	25 minutes	50 minutes

You can use sushi rice to make risotto if you don't have Arborio rice on hand. Both types of rice have a similar grain size and starch level, so they're pretty interchangeable. When I discovered that, I thought it would be fun to make arancini from the sushi rice to give some sushi rolls a little salty crunch.

SUSHI MASTER➡ For this recipe, I grab precut fish at a local Asian market, but feel free to buy a larger piece of raw fish if you have a sharp knife and the skills to make proper sushi cuts.

½ cup sushi rice

salt

1 tablespoon rice vinegar

1 pinch sugar

canola or peanut oil for frying

1 cup panko breadcrumbs

wasabi

Sriracha

12 slices sushi-grade raw fish

chives

soy sauce

1. Rinse the rice in a mesh strainer until the water runs clear.

2. Place the rice in a small pot with 1 cup of water and a little salt. Bring to a simmer, cover, and reduce the heat to low. Cook for about 20 minutes.

3. Remove from the heat and allow to sit for 10 minutes.

4. Pour the cooked rice into a bowl and add the vinegar, sugar, and a pinch of salt. Mix well and continue to stir and mix for about 15 minutes, until the mixture comes to room temperature. Try doing this in front of a fan or outside in cold weather.

5. Preheat the oil to 375°F.

6. Place the breadcrumbs on a plate.

7. Form the rice into 6 balls and press each into the breadcrumbs to coat.

8. Fry the rice balls for 3 to 5 minutes, until brown. Remove from the heat and allow to cool on a rack. Immediately season with salt.

9. When the balls have cooled, break each in half by sticking a knife in the center and gently prying it apart.

10. Place a dot each of wasabi and Sriracha on the rice, top with a piece of fish, and sprinkle with chives.

11. Serve with soy sauce for dipping.

BREADSTICK CALZONES

MAKES	PREP TIME	COOK TIME	TOTAL TIME
12 calzones	25 minutes	35 minutes	1 hour
	(more if making dough)		

One Italian chain restaurant started serving sandwiches on their acclaimed breadsticks. I thought it would be fun to take it one step further and bake the sandwich into the breadstick. I use sausage, peppers, and onions, as with a classic calzone, but you can use salami, pepperoni, prosciutto, or other ingredients you like in a calzone.

1. Lightly coat a clean counter with flour. Place the dough on the counter and allow it to come to room temperature.

2. In a pan, cook the peppers and onions on medium heat with the olive oil until they soften and reduce in size, about 10 minutes.

3. Remove sausage meat from the casing and add to the pan. Cook 10 minutes, until cooked through and crumbled. Remove from heat.

4. Coat a half sheet pan with oil and preheat the oven to 350°F.

5. Split the dough in half.

6. Roll out one of the halves on the counter into a very thin rectangle, about 12 × 14 inches.

7. Cut the dough lengthwise into 6 strips.

8. Place a little of the mozzarella and the sausage mixture onto each strip of dough. Roll the dough tightly lengthwise into a long breadstick, sealing it at both ends.

9. Put the breadstick, seam side down, onto the baking sheet and repeat with the remaining strips of dough.

10. Repeat steps 6 through 9 with the other half of the dough.

11. Sprinkle Parmesan cheese over the breadsticks and allow them to rise for 15 minutes.

12. Bake for 15 minutes, until browned on top, but be careful that they don't explode.

13. Serve with heated marinara sauce for dipping.

all-purpose flour for dusting

1 batch pizza dough (page 179 or store bought)

½ small red pepper, diced

½ small yellow onion, diced

1 tablespoon olive oil, plus more for the pan

¼ pound hot Italian sausage

1 cup grated mozzarella cheese

¼ cup grated Parmesan cheese

1 cup marinara sauce (page 177 or store bought)

PIZZA STICKY BUNS

MAKES	PREP TIME	COOK TIME	TOTAL TIME
8 buns	45 minutes (more if making dough)	25 minutes	1 hour 10 minutes

My mom used to make pepperoni bread for my sisters and me, when we were growing up, as a snack. It was one of the first dishes I learned to make, and I put it into my first cookbook. When Pizza Sticky Buns made the rounds on the Internet, I thought it was funny that they were basically pizza bread with a twist, so I came up with this recipe.

all-purpose flour for dusting

1 batch pizza dough (page 179 or store bought)

3 cups marinara sauce (page 177 or store bought), divided use

¼ pound thin-sliced provolone

½ pound thin-sliced pepperoni

2 cups shredded mozzarella cheese

1. Lightly dust a clean counter with flour. Place the dough on the counter and allow it to come to room temperature.

2. Preheat the oven to 350°F.

3. Pour 1 cup of the sauce into a 5 × 9-inch baking dish.

4. Roll the dough out to a 12 × 16-inch rectangle.

5. Spread a thin layer of marinara sauce on the dough.

6. Cover the sauce with a layer of provolone.

7. Add a layer of pepperoni.

8. Top with the shredded mozzarella.

9. Roll the dough in a cylinder, widthwise, so you end up with a 16-inch-long roll, then cut it into 2-inch sections.

10. Gently coat each section with marinara sauce, then place into the prepared baking dish, spiral facing up. All 8 should fit snugly in the pan.

11. Allow to rise for 30 minutes.

12. Top with the remaining marinara sauce.

13. Bake for 25 minutes, until puffy and brown.

BUFFALO CAULIFLOWER KOREAN PANCAKES

MAKES	PREP TIME	COOK TIME	TOTAL TIME
2 (5-inch) pancakes	45 minutes	16 minutes	61 minutes

Buffalo cauliflower used to substitute as a vegetarian take on buffalo chicken, but it has become so popular that it's its own thing now. Most people are familiar with scallion pancakes, but the Korean version is a lot chunkier, with loads of spicy and funky kimchi and a crispy crust. I swapped the kimchi for cauliflower marinated in tart and spicy buffalo sauce, so it still recalls the pancake that inspired it.

1 cup chopped cauliflower

¼ cup chopped carrots, plus more for serving

¼ cup chopped celery, plus more for serving

¼ cup cayenne hot sauce

1 tablespoon melted butter

salt and pepper

½ cup all-purpose flour

1 tablespoon vegetable oil

blue cheese dressing

1. In a large bowl, mix the cauliflower, carrots, celery, hot sauce, and melted butter with a pinch of salt and pepper and allow to marinate on the counter for 30 minutes.

2. Mix the flour into the cauliflower mixture, along with as much water as needed to form a thick batter, about ¼ cup.

3. Preheat a small frying pan on high with a light coating of the vegetable oil and add half of the cauliflower mixture to it.

4. Cook each pancake for about 4 minutes per side to brown and cook through.

5. Serve with blue cheese dressing and fresh carrots and celery.

 THE INGREDIENTS OF BUFFALO CAULIFLOWER COMBINED WITH ➡  THE INGREDIENTS OF A KOREAN PANCAKE MAKE ➡  New Mash-up! BUFFALO CAULIFLOWER KOREAN PANCAKES

CHEESEBURGER ONION RINGS

MAKES	PREP TIME	COOK TIME	TOTAL TIME
20 rings	1 hour 30 minutes	15 minutes	1 hour 45 minutes

I've wanted to stuff onion rings for years, but it seemed complicated and impossible to photograph properly. The process turned out much easier than expected, though, and these onion rings are one of my favorite bites of food in this whole book.

FOR THE CHEESE SNOBS ➡ You can use a more natural cheese for the sauce and make a roux or a cornstarch sauce, but natural cheese more easily separates when heated with the acidity from the pickles and ketchup. Because of this, I opted for processed. The consistency and flavor of the resulting sauce are absolutely perfect for this dish.

RINGS

2 large white onions

½ pound ground beef

canola or peanut oil for frying

1 cup all-purpose flour, plus more for dredging

1 tablespoon paprika

1 egg

1 cup light beer, plus more if needed

salt and pepper

SAUCE

6 ounces processed easy-melting cheese (such as Velveeta)

¼ cup chopped pickles

1 tablespoon pickle juice

2 tablespoons ketchup

1. Slice the onions into ½-inch rounds.

2. Carefully separate the rings from one of the rounds, keeping them in order of largest to smallest. Place the largest, second largest, and third largest next to one another. Place the fourth largest inside the first, the fifth inside the second, and the sixth inside the third.

3. Tightly pack ground beef between the rings. Set the finished rings aside and continue with the remaining rings.

4. Allow the assembled rings to chill for at least 1 hour before cooking.

5. Preheat frying oil to 375°F.

6. In a mixing bowl, combine the flour and paprika. Put some additional flour on a plate for dredging the rings.

7. Whisk the egg and beer into the flour in the bowl, adding additional beer if needed to form a thin batter.

8. Season the onion rings with salt and pepper.

9. One by one, dredge the rings in the flour and then dip into the batter using a fork. Allow extra batter to drop off the rings and then drop them into the hot oil.

10. Fry the rings in batches for about 3 to 5 minutes each, until golden brown. Allow to cool on a rack and season with additional salt and pepper.

11. To make the sauce, chop the cheese into cubes and add them along with the remaining sauce ingredients to a microwave-safe bowl.

12. Microwave on high for 15 seconds. Stir and repeat until melted and creamy.

13. Serve the rings with the sauce.

THE INGREDIENTS OF A CHEESEBURGER
COMBINED WITH

THE INGREDIENTS OF ONION RINGS
MAKE

New Mash-up!

CHEESEBURGER ONION RINGS

SHRIMP & GRITS HUSH PUPPIES

MAKES	PREP TIME	COOK TIME	TOTAL TIME
15 hush puppies	3 hours 15 minutes	45 minutes	4 hours

Grits and polenta really solidify the day after you cook them, which inspired this recipe. If you work quickly at the right time, you can use hardened grits as a coating for fried shrimp and create a handheld bite of shrimp and grits. These also remind me of the stuffed shrimp that my family serves at Christmas—a bonus mash-up.

1. Pour the stock into a heavy-bottomed pot and bring to a simmer.

2. Whisk in the grits and reduce the heat to low. Season heavily with salt and pepper.

3. Simmer the grits, stirring often, for about 25 minutes.

4. Stir in the butter, cheese, parsley, and lemon juice. Pour the mixture into a baking dish and allow to cool on the counter for 10 minutes.

5. One by one, dredge a shrimp in the flour, then pack grits around it to cover it fully. Press hard to seal it well. Place the coated shrimp onto a lightly greased plate or baking dish. Repeat with the remaining shrimp.

6. Chill in the refrigerator for at least 3 hours or overnight.

7. Preheat the oil to 350°F.

8. Fry shrimp in batches of 5 (or however many fit in your fryer) for about 5 minutes each, until the grits turn golden brown and the shrimp fully cook.

9. Serve with cocktail sauce.

3½ cups vegetable stock

1 cup stone ground grits

salt and pepper

2 tablespoons butter

4 ounces shredded Cheddar cheese

¼ cup chopped parsley

juice of 1 lemon

15 jumbo shrimp, peeled and deveined, tails on

all-purpose flour for dredging

canola or peanut oil for frying

cocktail sauce

CHEESESTEAK CHEESECAKES

MAKES	PREP TIME	COOK TIME	TOTAL TIME
4 (4-inch) cheesecakes or 1 (9-inch) cheesecake	5 minutes	1 hour 30 minutes	1 hour 35 minutes

Savory cheesecake may not sound tasty at first, but it's great to serve at or bring to a party. It works well as a replacement for a spreadable cheese or baked brie and goes well with crackers or bread. This version uses Philly cheesesteak as the flavor inspiration, with provolone and American cheeses, lots of banana peppers—essential to a good cheesesteak—and sweet caramelized onion jam on top.

SERVING TEMPERATURE➡ Serve this dish at just a bit above room temperature. You can make it early, keep it in the fridge, then heat it in the oven at 250°F for 15 minutes before serving.

4 tablespoons butter, divided, plus more for greasing

2 large yellow onions, sliced thin

1 tablespoon red wine vinegar

1 pinch sugar

1½ cups plain breadcrumbs

olive oil

½ pound thin sliced rib eye steak

¼ cup chopped banana peppers

8 ounces cream cheese

6 ounces provolone cheese

4 ounces American cheese

2 eggs

¼ cup whole milk

1. Add 2 tablespoons of the butter to a nonstick frying pan along with the onions. Cook on medium heat for about 25 minutes, until golden brown.

2. Add the vinegar and sugar and cook an additional 10 minutes to achieve a jamlike consistency.

3. Preheat the oven to 350°F.

4. Melt the remaining 2 tablespoons of butter and stir it into the breadcrumbs.

5. Grease the pan(s) with butter and press the breadcrumb mixture into the bottom to form a crust. Bake for 10 minutes to help seal and form the crust.

6. Meanwhile, in a frying pan with a splash of olive oil, cook the meat on high heat for about 8 minutes, stirring often, to brown. Stir in the banana peppers.

7. In a food processor, mix the cheeses, eggs, and milk and pulse until well combined.

8. Add the meat mixture to the food processor and pulse a few more times.

9. Pour the cheesecake mixture into the pan(s) gently so you don't disturb the crust. Bake for about 40 minutes for smaller pans or 50 minutes for one large pan. Allow to cool before serving.

CORN DOG JALAPEÑO POPPERS

MAKES	PREP TIME	COOK TIME	TOTAL TIME
10 poppers	20 minutes	15 minutes	35 minutes

Jalapeño poppers and corn dogs have a lot in common already, so it was obvious to me to put them together. It was as easy as putting a hot dog into the popper, and then instead of normal breading, using cornmeal batter. The foods in this combo go great together, and if a food truck started selling these at a state fair, they would be the highlight of the entire event.

1. Cut the top and bottom off each jalapeño. Use a small knife to remove the seeds and hollow out the jalapeños.

2. Cut the hot dogs in half lengthwise and then into thirds so you have 6 half-cylinders from each hot dog that are about the same length as the jalapeños. Trim the peppers if needed.

3. Mix the cream cheese, hot sauce, and cumin and stir well to combine.

4. Push a hot dog piece inside each pepper, then fill the pepper with the cream cheese mixture. Use a thin knife to push the cream cheese into the center and uniformly fill the jalapeño. Pack it tightly.

5. Mix the cornmeal, flour, baking powder, salt, and pepper in a large bowl. Stir in the egg and buttermilk and mix until it just comes together.

6. Preheat the oil to 375°F.

7. Place the dredging flour on a plate and add a little salt.

8. Coat each jalapeño with a thin layer of oil, then use a fork to dip it into the cornmeal batter.

9. Gently drop it into the fryer and repeat until the fryer is full. Don't overcrowd. Fry the poppers for about 5 minutes, or until they set and start to brown.

10. Remove the poppers from the oil, drain them on a rack, and immediately sprinkle them with a little more salt. Repeat with the next batch of poppers if needed.

11. Serve with mustard.

10 large jalapeño peppers

2 hot dogs

8 ounces cream cheese

1 tablespoon hot sauce

½ teaspoon cumin

1 cup cornmeal

1 cup all-purpose flour, plus more for dredging

2 teaspoons baking powder

2 teaspoons salt, plus more to taste

1 teaspoon black pepper

1 egg

1 cup buttermilk

canola or peanut oil for frying and coating

mustard

FESENJOON CHICKEN WINGS

MAKES	PREP TIME	COOK TIME	TOTAL TIME
24 wings	6 hours 15 minutes	35 minutes	6 hours 50 minutes

Fesenjoon is a Persian stew made from chicken, walnuts, and pomegranate juice. A friend's mom made it as part of a Persian feast, and I freaked out over how amazing it tasted. I've played around with this flavor combination in a handful of dishes, but these wings are the best by far. The stew flavors become a sticky glaze for the wings, which are topped with walnuts, pomegranate seeds, and parsley.

1. Marinate the wings in the yogurt, salt, pepper, turmeric, and cinnamon for at least 6 hours or overnight.

2. Mix the tzatziki ingredients and store in the fridge until ready to use.

3. In a medium frying pan, cook the onion with the olive oil on medium heat for about 5 minutes. Add the chicken stock and cook another 5 minutes. Add the pomegranate juice and honey and simmer for 15 to 20 minutes to reduce to a thick glaze.

4. Preheat the frying oil to 375°F.

5. Lightly toast the walnuts on medium heat for 3 to 5 minutes. Keep a close eye on them because they can burn easily and immediately remove to a plate to cool.

6. Remove the wings from the yogurt and shake off the excess. Lightly coat the wings in rice flour.

7. Fry the wings for about 8 minutes, until very crispy.

8. After frying, immediately put the wings into the glaze and toss to coat.

9. Top with the toasted walnuts, parsley, and pomegranate seeds and serve with the tzatziki for dipping.

WINGS

24 wings

1 cup yogurt

salt and pepper

1 tablespoon turmeric

½ teaspoon cinnamon

TZATZIKI

1 cup yogurt

½ cup minced cucumber

¼ cup finely chopped parsley

1 small clove garlic, grated

juice of 1 lemon

1 teaspoon honey

1 pinch salt

SAUCE & TOPPINGS

¼ cup minced white onion

1 tablespoon olive oil

½ cup chicken stock

16 ounces pomegranate juice

2 tablespoons honey

canola or peanut oil for frying

½ cup diced walnuts

rice flour for dredging

¼ cup chopped parsley

½ cup pomegranate seeds

MALAI KOFTA ARANCINI

MAKES	PREP TIME	COOK TIME	TOTAL TIME
10 arancini	4 hours 15 minutes	45 minutes	5 hours

Malai kofta are tasty fried dumplings of cheese and potato served in a creamy curry sauce often with rice on the side. They're also one of my favorite Indian takeout meals. I decided to put the rice and sauce inside the dumpling, and making it as a risotto was the best way to achieve this perfect mash-up.

1. In a heavy-bottomed pot or Dutch oven on medium-high heat, add the oil and cook the onion for about 10 minutes, until it starts to brown around the edges.

2. Add the rice and potato and cook for 5 minutes, stirring to combine.

3. Add the garlic, ginger, and chiles and cook for 3 minutes.

4. Add the curry powder and cook for 2 minutes

5. Add 1 cup of the stock and stir well, scraping the bottom of the pan to get any browned bits off the bottom.

6. Continue adding the stock 1 cup at a time when the rice mixture looks dry.

7. Cook until the rice is tender, stirring often, adding water if you run out of stock.

8. When the rice is tender, stir in the cheese.

9. Remove from the heat and allow to cool. Transfer to a sealable container and refrigerate at least 4 hours but preferably overnight.

10. Preheat the frying oil to 375°F.

11. Place the breadcrumbs on a plate.

12. Form balls with the hardened arancini.

13. Press the balls into the breadcrumbs so the crumbs stick.

14. Fry for about 5 minutes, until golden brown.

INGREDIENTS

1 tablespoon olive oil

1 small yellow onion, diced

½ cup Arborio rice

1 large russet potato, diced

2 cloves garlic, minced

1 inch ginger, minced

3 fresh red or green Thai chiles, minced

1 tablespoon curry powder (page 176 or store bought)

4 cups vegetable stock, divided

1 cup crumbled paneer cheese

canola or peanut oil for frying

2 cups plain breadcrumbs

salt and pepper

CILANTRO CHUTNEY

1 bunch cilantro, stems and leaves, cleaned and roughly chopped

1 teaspoon grated ginger

1 fresh red or green Thai chile, chopped, seeds optional

juice of 1 lime

1 pinch cumin

salt and pepper

**THE INGREDIENTS
OF <u>MALAI KOFTA</u>
COMBINED WITH**

↓

**THE INGREDIENTS
OF <u>ARANCINI</u>
MAKE**

↓

New
Mash-up!

MALAI KOFTA ARANCINI

15. Immediately season with salt and pepper and allow to cool on a rack.

16. Place all the chutney ingredients in a food processor and process until smooth.

17. Serve the arancini with the chutney for dipping.

REUBEN TOTS

MAKES	PREP TIME	COOK TIME	TOTAL TIME
6 servings	30 minutes	15 minutes	45 minutes

Putting things onto tots is a great way of making mash-ups. This Reuben sandwich version didn't make it into my tater tots book, but I love it—so here it is.

STORE-BOUGHT VS. HOMEMADE ➡ You can buy Russian dressing, but it's easy and fun to make your own, and you probably have all the ingredients at home already. If you want to go totally scratch on this one, you can make the corned beef, sauerkraut, and even the tots, but store-bought works just as well for those.

1. Preheat the oven to 450°F.

2. Gently toss the frozen tots in the olive oil and salt.

3. Bake the tots for 25 minutes, flipping once during cooking, until brown and crispy.

4. Meanwhile, mix the Russian dressing ingredients to make the dressing.

5. Pile the tots in a baking dish, layering them like nachos with the corned beef, sauerkraut, and cheese. Top with cheese.

6. Bake for about 15 minutes to melt and lightly brown the cheese.

7. Serve with the Russian dressing for dipping.

INGREDIENTS

60 tots

3 tablespoons olive oil

1 pinch salt

¼ pound corned beef, chopped and shredded

1 cup sauerkraut

1 cup grated Gruyère cheese

RUSSIAN DRESSING

½ cup mayonnaise

1 tablespoon ketchup

1 tablespoon Sriracha

¼ cup finely chopped pickles

1 tablespoon prepared horseradish

1 teaspoon Worcestershire sauce

¼ teaspoon paprika

THE INGREDIENTS OF A REUBEN SANDWICH COMBINED WITH ➡

THE INGREDIENTS OF A TATER TOTS MAKE ➡

New Mash-up! REUBEN TOTS

BLT STEAMED BUN SLIDERS

MAKES	PREP TIME	COOK TIME	TOTAL TIME
10 sliders	30 minutes	4 hours 30 minutes	5 hours

When you make pork belly right, it's just a thicker, juicier piece of bacon. One day, I was having pork belly steamed buns at an Asian restaurant, and it reminded me of a BLT sandwich. I ran with the idea and mashed up the two sandwiches to make this perfectly fluffy, juicy, intensely flavorful slider.

GRAB YOUR BUNS ➡ This recipe becomes extremely easy if you buy steamed buns instead of making them. No shame! I do it most of the time. You can find them in the freezer section of almost any Asian market.

PORK

1. Preheat the oven to 300°F.

2. Slice the pork belly into 10 strips, mix with the remaining pork belly ingredients in a large bowl, and stir well.

3. Pour into a shallow baking dish or oven-safe frying pan and bake for about 4 hours, flipping occasionally, until tender, sticky, and brown on the edges.

DOUGH

4. In a mixing bowl, stir the yeast, sugar, and oil together with ½ cup warm water and set aside for 10 minutes, until the yeast activates.

5. Stir in the flour and salt and knead the mixture for about 10 minutes, until it's no longer sticky and becomes smooth and elastic. I do this with my hands, but a stand mixer works great, too.

6. Cover the dough. Let it sit for about 1 hour, until it doubles in size.

7. Spread some flour on a work surface. Split the dough into 10 balls. Roll each ball into an oval and coat in flour. Fold it over into a half circle in a traditional bun shape.

8. Repeat with the remaining dough balls and allow them to sit on the counter for 20 minutes to rise again.

PORK BELLY

2 pounds boneless skinless pork belly

¼ cup sesame oil

¼ cup soy sauce

½ cup rice vinegar

¼ cup sambal chile paste

2 cloves garlic

1 tablespoon smoked paprika

2 tablespoons honey

BUNS

1 packet active dry yeast

2 tablespoons sugar

2 tablespoons vegetable oil

2 cups all-purpose flour, plus more for dusting

1 teaspoon salt

SANDWICH

⅓ cup mayonnaise

¼ cup Sriracha

1 heart romaine lettuce, chopped

2 tomatoes, sliced

THE INGREDIENTS OF
A BLT SANDWICH
COMBINED WITH

↓

THE INGREDIENTS
OF **STEAMED BUNS**
MAKE

↓

New
Mash-up!

BLT STEAMED BUN SLIDERS

9. Preheat the steamer and add the buns 3 or 4 at a time. Each batch will take about 15 minutes.

SANDWICH

10. In a small bowl, mix the mayonnaise and Sriracha.

11. Build the sandwiches, starting with the mayonnaise mixture on the bottom, then lettuce, followed by a slab of pork belly, and a tomato slice on top.

NASHVILLE HOT CHICKEN PIEROGI

MAKES	PREP TIME	COOK TIME	TOTAL TIME
4 servings	1 hour 50 minutes	25 minutes	2 hours 15 minutes

I helped plan an event at which a Polish folk singer was performing some songs a week before moving to Nashville. His life and songs inspired me to create a few recipes, one being this Polish-Nashville "nash-up."

SLAW

1. Mix all the slaw ingredients and refrigerate for at least 1 hour.

CHICKEN TENDERS

2. Toss the chicken with salt and pepper and refrigerate for 1 hour.

3. Bring frying oil to 375°F.

4. In a shallow bowl, beat the eggs with the hot sauce. Pour 1 cup of flour into another shallow bowl and season with more salt and pepper.

5. Add remaining ½ cup of flour to the chicken and toss to coat. Each piece should have a light coating.

6. In groups of 3 or so, dip the chicken pieces in the egg wash to coat and then toss in the flour mixture. Set pieces aside on a plate until they all have been coated.

7. Fry the chicken in batches of 6 to 10 pieces (depending on the size of your fryer) for 8 minutes. Don't overcrowd.

8. Drain the chicken on a wire rack.

9. Meanwhile, in a metal bowl, mix the cayenne pepper, brown sugar, paprika, and garlic powder.

10. Very carefully spoon ½ cup of the hot frying oil into the spice mixture. Be careful not to breath in too deeply during this process! Whisk to combine.

11. Dip the chicken pieces into the spicy oil and return them to the rack.

SLAW

½ head cabbage, sliced very thin

2 carrots, julienned or spiralized

3 red Fresno chile peppers, sliced very thin

3 tablespoons sour cream

juice of 1 lime

salt and pepper

HOT CHICKEN TENDERS

1 pound chicken tenders

salt and pepper

oil for frying

2 eggs

1 tablespoon hot sauce

1½ cups flour

1 tablespoon cayenne pepper or more

1 tablespoon brown sugar

½ tablespoon paprika

1 teaspoon garlic powder

20 dill pickle slices

CONTINUED ➡

12. Pour the flour into a large bowl.

13. In another bowl, mix the sour cream, butter, and egg until they combine.

14. Pour the liquid into the flour and mix well. Start kneading when it becomes too thick to stir.

15. Knead, adding more flour if needed, until the dough forms. Allow to rest for 30 minutes.

16. On a well-floured countertop, roll the dough out to about ⅛-inch thick.

17. Cut the dough into about 2-inch rounds. Use the rim of a glass if you don't have a round dough cutter.

18. Chop the chicken into small pieces and place into a bowl.

19. Chop the pickles and add to the chicken. Stir to combine.

20. One by one, fill the rounds with the chicken filling, putting a good ¼ cup of filling into each round.

21. Fold the dough in half over the filling to form a half moon. Use a little water to seal the dough, then pinch the ends with a fork to make it tight.

22. Boil the pierogi for about 4 minutes until they start floating.

23. Strain them out and place directly into a frying pan with some melted butter. Cook to brown on both sides, about 3 minutes each side.

24. Serve the pierogi with the slaw.

PIEROGI DOUGH

3 cups flour, plus more for dusting

½ cup sour cream

¼ cup butter, plus more for browning

1 egg

THE INGREDIENTS OF HOT WINGS COMBINED WITH ➡

THE INGREDIENTS OF PIEROGI MAKE ➡

New Mash-up!

NASHVILLE HOT CHICKEN PIEROGI

DIPS

BLT GUACAMOLE

MAKES	PREP TIME	COOK TIME	TOTAL TIME
4 to 6 servings	30 minutes	5 minutes	35 minutes

Putting avocado in a BLT is pretty much standard now. It even has its own name, the BLAT. (If you put the A in any other spot in that acronym, you're wrong.) Making guacamole with extra tomatoes, a little chopped arugula, and crispy chewy bacon hints at the BLAT, but serving it with toast as the dipper drives home the point.

5 slices thick-cut bacon

3 avocados

salt and pepper

juice of 1 lime

½ small yellow onion, diced finely

1 jalapeño pepper, seeds removed, diced

1 clove garlic, grated

2 vine-ripened tomatoes, diced, divided

1 cup chopped arugula

8 slices sourdough bread

1. Cook the bacon until crisp. Break into bite-size pieces, chop and set aside.

2. Peel and pit the avocados and place in a large bowl. Season with salt and pepper and add the lime juice.

3. Add the onion, jalapeño, and garlic and stir to combine.

4. Reserve some of the chopped tomato and bacon for garnish and stir in the rest along with the arugula.

5. Top the guacamole with the reserved tomato and bacon.

6. Toast the bread, cut each slice into quarters, and serve with the guacamole as dippers.

THE INGREDIENTS OF A BLT SANDWICH COMBINED WITH ➡

THE INGREDIENTS OF GUACAMOLE MAKE ➡

New Mash-up!
BLT GUACAMOLE

LAMB GYRO DIP

MAKES	PREP TIME	COOK TIME	TOTAL TIME
8 servings	1 hour 15 minutes	30 minutes	1 hour 45 minutes

I've always loved the idea of turning a sandwich into a dip. So much of what we dip into dips is bread, so it makes a lot of sense. This gyro dip is one of my favorite iterations of the sandwich-as-dip concept. It's a glorified tzatziki, but by adding meat, spices, and tomatoes it suddenly becomes a gyro in every bite.

1. In a frying pan, heat the olive oil on medium heat and sauté the onion for about 15 minutes to brown.

2. When the onion just starts browning, add the lamb. Cook until the meat browns, about 10 minutes, removing fat if needed.

3. Add the oregano, cumin, and sumac and cook another 5 minutes. Remove from the heat and let cool slightly.

4. Meanwhile, in a bowl, mix together the yogurt, cucumbers, tomato, dill, garlic, and lemon juice, reserving a few pieces of cucumber, tomato, and dill for garnish.

5. Combine the lamb and yogurt mixtures, adding more yogurt as needed. Refrigerate for 1 hour or so before serving.

6. Top the dip with the reserved cucumber, tomato, and dill and serve with pita chips.

1 tablespoon olive oil

½ small yellow onion, diced

½ pound ground lamb

2 teaspoons oregano

1 teaspoon cumin

1 teaspoon sumac

1½ cup yogurt, plus more if needed

½ cup diced cucumbers

½ cup diced tomato

¼ cup minced dill

1 clove garlic, grated or pressed

juice of 1 lemon

pita chips

THE INGREDIENTS OF LAMB GYROS COMBINED WITH ➡

THE INGREDIENTS OF TSATZIKI MAKE ➡

New Mash-up! LAMB GYRO DIP

LEMON ASPARAGUS RISOTTO DIP

MAKES	PREP TIME	COOK TIME	TOTAL TIME
8 servings	5 minutes	45 minutes	50 minutes

When I first made risotto as a dip, I was shocked at how well it worked. It was cheesy, creamy, and everything you want in a good dip. To make this a true comfort food mash-up, though, it needed a common risotto, so I went with a lemon asparagus variety.

SOUPY NOT STICKY➡ One of the keys to any risotto—and this dip especially—is that the mixture should be saucy and soupy rather than tight and dry. Err on the side of extra liquid and you'll be in good shape. You want it easily dippable.

1 large white onion, diced

2 tablespoons olive oil

2 cloves garlic, minced

1 cup Arborio rice

1 cup vegetable stock

10 asparagus stalks

1 quart whole milk

8 ounces crumbled feta cheese

1 tablespoon chopped fresh thyme

juice of 2 lemons

pita bread, toasted

1. Sauté the onion in the olive oil on high heat until it lightly browns around the edges, stirring often, about 10 minutes.

2. Add the garlic and rice. Stir to coat the rice in oil and lightly toast, about 2 minutes.

3. Add the stock and stir. Cook until the stock evaporates a little, about 8 minutes.

4. Chop the asparagus spears into small rounds and add them to the mixture.

5. Add the milk 1 cup at a time, stirring often, as the rice cooks. Each time you add milk, stir and cook the risotto until the milk has mostly absorbed and evaporated. This process should take about 25 minutes. If the rice isn't fully cooked when you run out of milk, continue the process using water.

6. Add the cheese, thyme, and lemon juice and remove from the heat. Stir to melt the cheese and mix well.

7. Serve warm with the toasted pita.

CHICKEN PICCATA DIP

MAKES	PREP TIME	COOK TIME	TOTAL TIME
4 servings	20 minutes	20 minutes	40 minutes

Even growing up in an Italian family, I had never heard of chicken piccata. In college, my roommate loved it—even though he picked around the capers. Buffalo chicken dip is popular, but I wanted to try that style with the flavors of chicken piccata. Leave the dip fairly thin in the baking dish so that the buttery breadcrumbs can get the attention they deserve.

1. In a frying pan on medium-high heat, melt the first third of the butter and brown the chicken on both sides, about 6 minutes per side. Remove the chicken from the pan.

2. Add the shallot and cook for about 5 minutes.

3. Meanwhile, preheat the oven to 350°F and shred the chicken with two forks.

4. Remove the pan from the heat and add the shredded chicken, capers, parsley, lemon juice, and the second third of the butter. Stir well to combine and allow the butter to melt. Stir in the cheese.

5. Pour the chicken mixture into a shallow baking dish.

6. Melt the final third of the butter and pour it into the breadcrumbs. Stir well to combine.

7. Top the chicken mixture with the breadcrumbs and bake for 20 minutes, until the breadcrumbs turn golden brown.

8. Serve with bread for dipping.

4 tablespoons butter, divided in thirds

8 ounces thin-sliced chicken breast

1 shallot, diced

¼ cup capers

¼ cup chopped parsley

juice of 2 lemons

½ cup grated Parmesan cheese

1 cup plain breadcrumbs

bread

THE INGREDIENTS OF CHICKEN PICATTA COMBINED WITH ➡

THE INGREDIENTS OF CHEESE DIP MAKE ➡

New Mash-up!

CHICKEN PICATTA DIP

Dip It Good!

Here's a selection of other dishes with great dip potential and how you might approach them.

Banh Mi → base: pâté and mayo
mix ins: pickled carrot and radish, cilantro, sriracha
dippers: baguette crostini

Chicken Parm → base: red sauce
mix ins: shredded chicken, parm, mozzarella
dippers: garlic rubbed crostini
(top with breadcrumbs and parm and bake)

Cuban Sandwich → base: cheese sauce
mix ins: pickles, ham, pork, mustard
dippers: toasted cuban bread

Everything Bagel
with Cream Cheese → base: cream cheese and sour cream
mix ins: everything spice, chives
dippers: bagel crisps

Pastrami Sandwich → base: cheese sauce
mix ins: pastrami, pickles, mustard
dippers: toasted rye

Pierogi → base: cheesy mash potatoes and sour cream
mix ins: bacon, chives, caramelized onions
dippers: fried pasta or endive

Stroganoff → base: sour cream
mix ins: steak, mushrooms, parsley
dippers: crostini

SOUPS & SANDWICHES

LAMB VINDALOO FRENCH ONION SOUP

MAKES	PREP TIME	COOK TIME	TOTAL TIME
8 bowls	5 minutes	2 hours 20 minutes	2 hours 25 minutes

A lot of the flavor of lamb vindaloo comes from deeply caramelized onions, which gave me the idea to mash it up with French onion soup. Adding meat to a soup makes it more of a meal rather than an appetizer. The lamb tastes perfectly tender, and the chiles give it a nice kick, but using naan instead of a baguette for the topping adds an extra surprise twist.

1. In a heavy-bottomed stock pot on high heat, cook the lamb in the olive oil. Brown it on all sides, about 15 minutes total, then remove it from the pot.

2. Add the onions and butter. This part takes a while and you need to watch it. Cook the onions on high heat for about 20 minutes, stirring fairly often and scraping the bottom of the pot to prevent too much sticking. Season with salt and pepper. The onions should reduce to about a quarter of their original volume and look nicely browned.

3. Add the broth, garlic, ginger, and chiles and cook for 2 minutes.

4. Add the garam masala, cumin, and curry powder and cook for 2 more minutes.

5. Add the lamb. Stir well and scrape the bottom of the pan to reincorporate any stuck bits. Simmer for 30 minutes.

6. Add the potatoes. Simmer for 1 hour, until the meat and potatoes become tender.

7. Pour into oven-safe bowls and cut the naan to the shape and size of the bowl.

8. Place the naan round on the top of the soup and top with cheese.

9. Broil for 5 to 10 minutes, depending on the strength of your broiler, to melt and brown the cheese lightly. Keep an eye on it to prevent burning.

1½ pounds lamb shoulder, cubed

2 tablespoons olive oil

7 onions, some white, some yellow, sliced

2 tablespoons butter

salt and pepper

2 quarts beef broth

3 cloves garlic, minced

2 inches ginger, minced

5 red Thai chiles, sliced into thin rounds

1 tablespoon garam masala (page 177 or store bought)

2 teaspoons cumin

1 teaspoon curry powder (page 176 or store bought)

2 large russet potatoes

2 tablespoons red vinegar

4 large pieces naan (page 178 or store bought)

8 ounces Gruyère cheese, grated

THAI COCONUT CLAM CHOWDER

MAKES	PREP TIME	COOK TIME	TOTAL TIME
5 servings	15 minutes	50 minutes	1 hour 5 minutes

This recipe mashes together the Thai soup tom kha and New England clam chowder, both white and creamy and two of my favorite soups. Turns out that bacon and coconut go really well together!

1. In a heavy-bottomed soup pot on medium-high heat, cook the bacon until crisp, about 5 minutes. Remove from the pot with a slotted spoon, leaving about half the bacon fat.

2. Add the butter and onion and cook for about 5 minutes to soften.

3. Add the garlic, ginger, chiles, cumin, and coriander. Cook 3 minutes.

4. Add the coconut milk, chicken stock, clam stock, potatoes, and lemongrass and stir to combine, scraping the bottom to incorporate any browned bits.

5. Strain the clam meat and add the juices to the pot. Set the clam meat aside.

6. Add the fish sauce and chile paste. Allow to simmer about 30 minutes, until the potatoes are perfectly tender.

7. Add the clam meat and cook for about 5 minutes, just until the meat firms slightly and is cooked. If you cook the mixture too long, the clams will become rubbery.

8. Remove from the heat and serve with lime wedges, chopped cilantro, and chile flakes.

¼ pound bacon, chopped

2 tablespoons butter

1 small yellow onion, diced

1 clove garlic, minced

2 inches ginger, grated

3 Thai chile peppers, minced

2 teaspoons cumin

2 teaspoons coriander

2 (13½-ounce) cans coconut milk

1 quart chicken stock

2 cups clam stock

3 Yukon Gold potatoes, peeled and diced

2 stalks lemongrass, cut into 1-inch pieces

1 pound fresh clam meat with juices or canned clams

1 tablespoon fish sauce

1 tablespoon chile paste

lime wedges for garnish

cilantro for garnish

chile flakes for garnish

CIOPPINO CHILI

MAKES	PREP TIME	COOK TIME	TOTAL TIME
10 servings	1 hour	30 minutes	2 hours and 15 minutes

In San Francisco, when I was eating cioppino—a big bowl of seafood stew cooked in tomato sauce—I realized that a few tweaks could turn it into a chili. The deep spice and flavor from the dried chiles go well with the fish, and the summer veggies give it a freshness that the original dish lacks.

CHILE STOCK AND SPICE BLEND

1. Remove the seeds from the chiles and place all of the chile stock ingredients into a pot with 2 cups of water. Bring to a boil, then remove from the heat. Allow to sit for 30 minutes, then blend to a smooth consistency.

2. Mix the spice blend ingredients.

VEGGIES

3. In another large pot on high heat, cook the onion, pepper, and zucchini in the olive oil to soften, about 10 minutes. Add the garlic and habaneros and cook for 1 minute. Add the prepared spice blend and cook for 1 more minute.

4. Add the tomato paste and cook for 2 to 3 minutes.

5. Add the blended chile stock, diced tomatoes, corn, and beans and simmer lightly for about 30 minutes while prepping the seafood.

SEAFOOD

6. Remove the beards from the scallops, scrape off any barnacles or fibers from the mussels, and peel, devein, and rinse the shrimp. Halve the scallops and cut up the shrimp and cod to match the size of the cut scallops. Cut the squid into rings.

7. In a separate pan, heat the white wine to a simmer. Add the mussels and cook, covered, for about 3 to 5 minutes, until they all open. If any don't open, throw them away.

CHILE STOCK

3 chipotle chiles

5 New Mexico chiles

3 ancho chiles

1 quart vegetable stock

1 clove garlic

SPICE BLEND

½ tablespoon cumin

½ teaspoon coriander

½ teaspoon mustard powder

1 pinch cinnamon

1 pinch cloves

VEGGIES

1 yellow onion, diced

1 green bell pepper, diced

1 zucchini, diced

2 tablespoons olive oil

2 cloves garlic, minced

3 habanero peppers, minced

6 ounces tomato paste

1 (28-ounce) can diced tomatoes

2 cups corn kernels

1 (15-ounce) can small white beans, strained and rinsed

CONTINUED ➡

8. Add the prepped seafood to the simmering chili. When the mussels have opened, add them to the chili along with the juices from the pan.

9. After about 2 to 5 minutes, the seafood will be cooked. Remove from the heat and serve with a garnish of cilantro.

SEAFOOD

½ pound bay scallops

2 pounds mussels

10 large shrimp

½ pound cod

3 squid, about ½ pound

1 cup white wine

cilantro for garnish

THE INGREDIENTS OF CIOPPINO COMBINED WITH ➡

THE INGREDIENTS OF CHILI MAKE ➡

New Mash-up!

CIOPPINO CHILI

ITALIAN WEDDING PANINI

MAKES	PREP TIME	COOK TIME	TOTAL TIME
4 sandwiches	30 minutes	20 minutes	50 minutes

My first idea for mashing Italian wedding soup into a sandwich was a meatball sub, but the flavors fit better in a panini. Think of this in the same vein as a grilled cheese sandwich served with tomato soup for dipping.

1. Mix the bread and milk and then mash them together.

2. Mix in the beef, pork, garlic, Parmesan cheese, parsley, and egg until everything combines, and then form the mixture into 1-inch meatballs.

3. In a frying pan, lightly brown the meatballs with the oil on medium heat, about 10 minutes.

4. Add the stock, Parmesan cheese, escarole (or spinach), and meatballs to a large saucepan and bring to a simmer. Cook for about 10 minutes, until the meatballs cook through.

5. Remove meatballs and escarole from the broth. Save the broth and cut the meatballs in half.

6. Build the sandwiches by stacking 1 slice of bread, 1 slice of mozzarella, 1 slice of provolone, meatball halves, escarole, 1 slice of provolone, and the other slice of bread.

7. On a grill or in a pan, cook the sandwiches with the butter or oil on medium heat. Cook on both sides to melt the cheese and brown the bread, 5 minutes per side.

8. Serve with a small cup of the cooking stock for dipping the sandwiches.

MEATBALLS

2 slices bread, crust removed

¼ cup whole milk

½ pound ground beef

½ pound ground pork

1 clove garlic, grated

½ cup grated Parmesan cheese

⅓ cup fresh parsley, chopped finely

1 egg

2 tablespoons olive oil

ESCAROLE

2 cups chicken stock

1 cup grated Parmesan cheese

1 pound fresh escarole or spinach

SANDWICHES

8 slices sourdough bread

4 thick slices mozzarella cheese

8 thick slices provolone

1 tablespoon butter or oil for grilling

CHANA GOBI MASALA FALAFEL SANDWICHES

MAKES	PREP TIME	COOK TIME	TOTAL TIME
4 to 6 sandwiches	9 hours 20 minutes	15 minutes	9 hours 35 minutes

Chana gobi masala is a chickpea and cauliflower curry and one of my favorite Indian dishes to make at home. One day I was imagining how it would taste without the liquid in the sauce, and it occurred to me that the whole mixture could be blended up and served as a falafel. With all the tweaks and curry powder, these taste like a great new take on falafel.

SUPER SOAKING➡ Soaked chickpeas aren't fully cooked the way that canned ones are. Soaking dried chickpeas will give them the distinct grainy falafel texture that you want.

1. In a food processor, pulse all the falafel ingredients except the oil until blended. Do not puree. You want small chunks of all the ingredients. Transfer the mixture to a bowl and refrigerate, covered, for at least 1 hour.

2. Mix all the salad ingredients and refrigerate.

3. Combine all the raita ingredients and refrigerate.

4. Preheat the frying oil to 350°F.

5. Form the falafel mixture into balls about the size of a table tennis ball. Fry for 5 minutes, until browned. Remove from oil and season with salt.

6. Build the sandwiches with pita, raita, salad, falafel, and lettuce.

FALAFEL

1½ cups dried chickpeas, soaked 8 hours or overnight

1 cup chopped cauliflower

1 small white onion, chopped

¼ cup cilantro, chopped

5 green Thai chiles, chopped (seeds optional)

2 cloves garlic

1 inch ginger, grated

1 tablespoon curry powder (page 176 or store bought)

1 teaspoon turmeric

1 teaspoon salt

1 teaspoon baking powder

¼ cup all-purpose flour

canola or peanut oil for frying

salt

SALAD

2 tomatoes, diced

1 small cucumber, diced

1 small red onion, diced

½ clove garlic, grated

¼ cup cilantro, chopped

salt and pepper

CONTINUED ➡

RAITA

1 cup Greek yogurt

2 tablespoons honey

½ cup cilantro

1 teaspoon cumin

salt and pepper

SANDWICH

pita bread

lettuce

THE INGREDIENTS OF <u>CHANA GOBI MASALA</u> COMBINED WITH ➡

THE INGREDIENTS OF <u>FALAFEL</u> MAKE ➡

New Mash-up!

CHANA GOBI MASALA FALAFEL

LOBSTER ROLL BANH MI

MAKES	PREP TIME	COOK TIME	TOTAL TIME
4 sandwiches	2 hours	5 minutes	2 hours 5 minutes

These sandwiches sparked a really interesting debate because people are purists about lobster. The whole state of Maine will shun you if you put an ounce of celery in a lobster roll! My friends loved these sandwiches but were a little preoccupied about the lobster not exactly being the star of the show—which makes sense when dealing with something as delicious and expensive as lobster. But no ingredient or dish is sacred, and I don't mind using lobster in fun, new, and creative ways.

1. To make the pickled carrot and radish mixture, cut the veggies and heavily salt them.

2. In a bowl, mix the vinegar with the sugar and teaspoon of salt and microwave on high for about 2 minutes. Pour the vinegar mixture over the veggies and let them sit for 1 hour or so before chilling them in the fridge. Once they have cooled, they are ready to use, but they're even better after a full day resting. Drain the veggies and rinse them.

3. Mix the coconut milk, mayo, fish sauce, and fresh mint. Put the lobster into a large bowl and add in the sauce—but be cautious. You don't want the lobster swimming in sauce. Start with about three-quarters of the sauce, and see how it looks. Add a little more as needed.

4. Lightly toast the baguettes on the outside.

5. Slice the baguettes three-quarters of the way through lengthwise, and scoop out a little of the bread to make room for the fillings.

6. Assemble the sandwich by adding the sliced cucumber, lobster, some cilantro, pickled carrots and radishes, and a few sliced chiles if you like it hot!

PICKLED CARROTS & RADISHES

1 cup julienned carrots

1 cup julienned radishes

salt

2 cups white vinegar

1 tablespoon sugar

1 teaspoon salt

1 clove garlic

LOBSTER SALAD

¾ cup coconut milk

¼ cup mayonnaise

2 tablespoons fish sauce

¼ cup mint, chopped

4 cups cooked lobster

SANDWICH

4 Vietnamese-style baguettes

1 small cucumber, sliced

cilantro

red and green Thai chile peppers (optional)

THAI SLOPPY JOES

MAKES	PREP TIME	COOK TIME	TOTAL TIME
6 sandwiches	10 minutes	15 minutes	25 minutes

I wrote this recipe as a simple way for a college kid to explore new flavors in the kitchen and enjoy Thai food—specifically pad ga prao—without having to order takeout. I loved it so much that I made a few tweaks and it's now one of my favorite recipes.

SLOW & LOW➡ The original version of this recipe was for a slow cooker, and it still works if you want to go that route. Add everything up to but not including the basil to the slow cooker, stir, and cook on high for 4 hours. Then stir in the basil and make the sandwiches.

1. In a large frying pan or wok on medium-high heat, cook the onion and pepper in the oil for 3 minutes, stirring.

2. Add the pork and turkey and cook for 2 minutes, stirring and breaking up the meat.

3. Add the green beans, fish sauce, soy sauce, sugar, sambal chile paste, and vinegar. Stir well to combine and simmer for 10 minutes.

4. Remove from the heat and stir in the basil.

5. To build the sandwich, load the bread with some cucumber and lettuce, then spoon in a nice helping of the meat.

1 white onion, sliced

1 red pepper, sliced

1 tablespoon olive oil

1 pound ground pork

1 pound ground turkey

1 cup chopped green beans

2 tablespoons fish sauce

1 tablespoon soy sauce

1 tablespoon sugar

¼ cup sambal chile paste

1 tablespoon rice vinegar

1 bunch fresh basil, chopped

6 sub rolls

sliced cucumber

shredded lettuce

THE INGREDIENTS OF <u>GAI GRA POW</u> COMBINED WITH ➡

THE INGREDIENTS OF A <u>SLOPPY JOE</u> MAKE ➡

New Mash-up!   THAI SLOPPY JOES

PO' BOY AREPAS

MAKES	PREP TIME	COOK TIME	TOTAL TIME
6 arepas	30 minutes	15 minutes	45 minutes

Arepas are so easy to make. They make a great bread for any sandwich, and they're gluten-free, so pretty much anyone can eat them. They work as po' boy bread because the cornmeal in the fish breading goes well with the corncake bread.

THIN FOR THE WIN➡ The biggest mistake when making arepas is making them too thick. Thin is always the way to go; otherwise they end up gummy or hard as concrete in the center. I like the Harina PAN® brand for the arepa flour.

1. Mix all the remoulade ingredients in a bowl. Refrigerate until ready to use.

2. Mix all the arepa ingredients in a bowl with 1½ cups of warm water. Add more water if needed. The dough should be fairly stiff and dry, similar to clay or Play-Doh®.

3. With your hands, form 6 thin rounds of the arepa dough, about 4 inches in diameter.

4. In a dry nonstick frying pan or cast iron skillet, cook the dough on high heat on both sides until areas of the arepas turn dark brown, about 5 minutes per side. Allow to cool.

5. For the catfish, preheat the oil to 350°F.

6. Mix the flour and cornmeal in a bowl.

7. Cut the fish into 2-inch nugget-sized chunks and season with salt, pepper, and paprika.

8. Dip the nuggets into the buttermilk and let the excess liquid drip off.

9. Dredge the nuggets in the flour and cornmeal mixture. Fry for 3 to 5 minutes, until they brown and cook through.

10. Cut the arepas in half, like an English muffin, to form the sandwich bread.

11. Spread remoulade on the bottom crust of the arepa, then add the fish, tomato, and lettuce.

REMOULADE

¾ cup mayonnaise

¼ cup Dijon mustard

juice of 1 lemon

1 tablespoon hot sauce

1 teaspoon Worcestershire sauce

1 scallion, chopped

1 tablespoon capers, chopped

1 clove garlic, grated

½ teaspoon paprika

AREPAS

2 cups arepa flour (par-cooked cornmeal)

1 egg

4 tablespoons melted butter

2 teaspoons salt

CATFISH

canola or peanut oil for frying

½ cup all-purpose flour

1 cup cornmeal

3 catfish fillets (about 8 ounces each)

salt and pepper

1 teaspoon paprika

1 cup buttermilk

sliced tomato

shredded lettuce

TACOS, NACHOS & BURRITOS

LASAGNA TACOS

MAKES	PREP TIME	COOK TIME	TOTAL TIME
20 mini tacos	15 minutes	1 hour 15 minutes	1 hour 30 minutes

Sometimes, when an idea for a new mash-up comes to me, it's so exciting that I have to make it the same day. This was one of those ideas. The lasagna ingredients translate to tacos so well. The sausage and sauce replace the taco meat and salsa, the ricotta replaces the sour cream, and the basil is the lettuce—so simple, so delicious.

DON'T GIVE UP➡ Frying the noodles into the taco shape takes a little practice. The noodles sometimes bubble up, stick to the tongs, or come loose. After a few tries, you'll get the hang of it. Use a fork to help get everything into the perfect shape.

½ pound lasagna noodles

2 hot Italian sausages

½ small yellow onion, diced

1 clove garlic, minced

1 (14-ounce) can diced tomatoes

canola or peanut oil for frying

1 cup ricotta cheese

10 leaves basil, chiffonade

1. Boil the noodles according to the package instructions, for about 10 minutes. Unlike with normal lasagna, you want to cook these fully.

2. Drain and cut the noodles into thirds and put them on a paper towel to dry.

3. Remove the casings from the sausages and crumble the meat. Then in a frying pan cook the sausage meat and onion over medium heat for about 5 minutes. Add the garlic, cook for 1 minute, and add the tomatoes. Simmer for about 10 minutes.

4. Heat the oil to 400°F.

5. One at a time, fold the lasagna squares into a nice taco shape and hold that shape with metal tongs as you dip it into the oil. Fry each square for about 3 minutes, until it's crispy and the bubbles have mostly stopped.

6. Assemble the tacos by layering the meat mixture into the bottom of the shell, followed by the ricotta and basil.

CHICKEN PANANG TACOS

MAKES	PREP TIME	COOK TIME	TOTAL TIME
12 tacos	30 minutes	45 minutes	1 hour 15 minutes

I have chicken panang curry and tofu drunken noodles from my local Thai place saved on speed dial in my phone. If it's been a long day or I need a night on the couch, one press of a button, and it shows up at my door. A fancier place served it with solid coconut cream on top that slowly melted into the dish, which reminded me of sour cream, so I ran with the idea for these tacos.

MAKE IT EASY➡ Tons of sites online can show you how to make great homemade panang curry paste, and making it yourself definitely makes this dish pop. It can be a lot of work and involves some exotic ingredients, though, so make this dish with the paste you can find at most grocery stores rather than not making it all. The lime leaf really makes the flavor of this dish. Use it if you can find it, but you can substitute a mixture of basil and mint, in which case use a little extra.

PASTE

1. Slice the tender part of the lemongrass stalks into chunks.

2. Roughly chop the chiles, shallots, garlic, ginger, cilantro stems, and peanuts.

3. Grind the spices if you're using whole spices.

4. Using either a mortar and pestle or food processor, add the ingredients one by one and pound or pulse until it each incorporates into the paste.

CHICKEN

5. Separate the coconut cream from the coconut milk by refrigerating for at least 8 hours, preferably overnight. When you open the cans, the thick white coconut cream will have floated to the top.

6. Spoon out 1 cup of the cream, divide it into 2 containers, and put it back into the fridge. Pour the rest of the contents of the 2 coconut milk cans into a large measuring cup or bowl.

CURRY PASTE

5 stalks lemongrass, fibrous outer leaves removed

7 red Thai chiles

5 shallots

5 cloves garlic

2 inches ginger

1 tablespoon cilantro stems

¼ cup peanuts

1 tablespoon chile flakes

1 tablespoon coriander

1 tablespoon cumin

1 teaspoon black pepper

CHICKEN

2 (14-ounce) cans coconut milk

2 pounds boneless skinless chicken thighs

3 stalks lemongrass, cut into 1-inch pieces

3 chunks grated galangal or ginger

3 lime leaves, or basil and mint

2 tablespoons fish sauce

1 tablespoon sugar

salt

CONTINUED ➡

7. In a medium pan, brown the chicken on high heat, about 5 minutes.

8. Add half of the coconut cream to the chicken. Once it melts, add the curry paste. Sauté for about 5 minutes, stirring constantly.

9. Add the coconut milk, lemongrass, galangal, lime leaves, fish sauce, and sugar. Salt to taste.

10. Simmer for about 45 minutes.

SLAW

11. Mix all the slaw ingredients and refrigerate.

TACOS

12. Mix the remaining half of the coconut cream with the lime juice.

13. Remove the lemongrass and galangal from the chicken.

14. Pour the chicken mixture into a bowl and shred the meat in the sauce.

15. Taste for seasoning and add more salt, sugar, or fish sauce as needed.

16. Brown the tortillas in a dry hot pan on high heat.

17. Build the tacos by layering the chicken first, then the slaw, followed by some coconut cream and a pinch of the lime leaf.

SLAW

1 English cucumber, sliced thin

1 red pepper, sliced thin

1 red Thai chile, diced

1 teaspoon sugar

juice of 1 lime

1 tablespoon fish sauce

TACOS

juice of 1 lime

2 lime leaves, sliced thin

10 soft corn tortillas

CARNE ASADA FRENCH FRY TACOS

MAKES	PREP TIME	COOK TIME	TOTAL TIME
12 tacos	1 hour	15 minutes	1 hour 15 minutes

Once I discovered carne asada fries, I tried them all over San Diego so I could create some cool recipes of my own. One of my ideas was to put the fries and all the toppings right into a taco. I worried that the fries might get lost in the taco, but the crunch of the shell mixed with the tender creamy potatoes and cheese makes these tacos unique and delicious.

STORE BOUGHT VS. HOMEMADE➡ Feel free to use frozen French fries for this dish. Just cook them according to the package instructions.

1. In a large bowl, mix the steak with all of the marinade ingredients. Marinate for 45 minutes. Set aside until ready to use.

2. Peel the potatoes and slice into fries. Rinse in cold water until the water runs clear. Soak in cold water for 45 minutes.

3. Heat the oil to 350°F. Fry potatoes in batches for about 8 minutes each to cook through. Remove from the oil and drain.

4. Bring the oil to 450°F. Fry potatoes in batches for about 3 minutes to crisp and brown. Remove from the oil and drain.

5. Mash the avocados and add ¼ cup of pico de gallo. Season with salt and pepper and refrigerate until ready to use.

6. Preheat the oven to 350°F.

7. On a grill or a cast iron grill pan, grill the steak on high heat about 6 minutes per side, to medium doneness.

8. Rest the steak at least 5 minutes before slicing it against the grain into thin strips.

9. Fill each taco shell with a few fries and top with cheese. Bake the loaded shells for 10 minutes.

10. Remove the shells from the oven and top with steak, guacamole, pico de gallo, and sour cream.

MARINATED MEAT

1 skirt steak, 1½ to 2 pounds

¼ cup olive oil

¼ cup Worcestershire sauce

2 tablespoons red wine vinegar

½ yellow onion, minced

2 cloves garlic, minced

1 tablespoon cumin

salt and pepper

FRIES

3 large russet potatoes

canola or peanut oil for frying

TACOS

2 avocados

2 cups pico de gallo (page 178 or store bought)

salt and pepper

12 crunchy shell tacos

2 cups shredded Cheddar cheese

1½ cups sour cream

GNOCCHOS

MAKES	PREP TIME	COOK TIME	TOTAL TIME
4 servings	15 minutes (1 hour if making gnocchi and taco meat)	15 minutes	30 minutes

When I was writing my tater tot cookbook, my brain fixated on "tot-cho" variations—ingredients I could dump on tots, nacho-style. Gnocchi are like soft little pillow tots, and this recipe was born.

1. Boil the gnocchi according to the package instructions. (If making them fresh, boil for about 5 minutes.) Drain and add the melted butter.

2. In a frying pan on high heat, add a splash of oil. Cook the gnocchi in batches to a golden brown.

3. Preheat the oven to 450°F.

4. On a baking sheet or cast iron pan, layer the gnocchi, cheese, pico de gallo, jalapeños, and taco meat.

5. Bake for about 15 minutes, until the cheese melts and starts to brown.

6. Top or serve with guacamole and sour cream.

40 gnocchi (page 177 or store bought)

2 tablespoons melted butter

1 tablespoon olive oil

1½ cups shredded Cheddar cheese

½ cup pico de gallo (page 178 or store bought)

15 slices pickled jalapeño peppers

½ cup cooked taco meat

guacamole

sour cream

 THE INGREDIENTS OF GNOCCHI COMBINED WITH ➡  THE INGREDIENTS OF NACHOS MAKE ➡  New Mash-up! GNOCCHOS

TOSTONE NACHOS

MAKES	PREP TIME	COOK TIME	TOTAL TIME
4 servings	25 minutes	15 minutes	40 minutes

Tostones done right are hot, crispy, salty, and delicious. They're amazing fresh from the fryer and dipped in a spicy-sour hot sauce, but serving them in nacho form puts a whole new spin on the dish. The tostones are definitely sturdy enough to hold the toppings and stay crispy underneath all that cheese.

HABANANA!➡ Habanana hot sauce is one of my signature recipes. I've been making it for a long time—we served it at my burrito shop, and I made it on *Guy's Grocery Games*. All the judges were choking. It's hot! This recipe makes plenty for you to keep in the fridge for a few weeks so you can put it on everything.

---

1. Blend all the hot sauce ingredients until smooth. Set aside until ready to use.

2. Peel the plantains and cut into 1-inch-thick rounds.

3. Fill a pan with 1 inch of oil and heat to 350°F.

4. Preheat the oven to 400°F.

5. Fry the plantains for about 5 minutes, until they just start to brown around the edges.

6. Remove the plantains from the oil and lightly salt. One by one, place the plantain rounds vertically on a cutting board and smash with a plate or another cutting board into the round tostone shape.

7. Heat the oil to 400°F and fry the smashed plantains in batches until crispy, about 5 minutes per batch.

8. Remove from the oil and season with salt.

9. In a baking dish or frying pan, build the nachos by layering the plantain chips with the carnitas and cheeses.

10. Bake for 10 minutes to melt the cheese.

11. Remove from the oven, top with the pico de gallo, and serve with the hot sauce.

HABANANA HOT SAUCE

5 bananas

10 habanero peppers, seeds removed

1 clove garlic

1 shallot

1 cup cilantro

juice of 3 limes

1 tablespoon red wine vinegar

salt

NACHOS

4 green plantains

canola or peanut oil for frying

salt

1 cup prepared carnitas (page 176 or store bought)

½ cup Monterey Jack cheese

½ cup Cheddar cheese

1½ cups pico de gallo (page 178 or store bought)

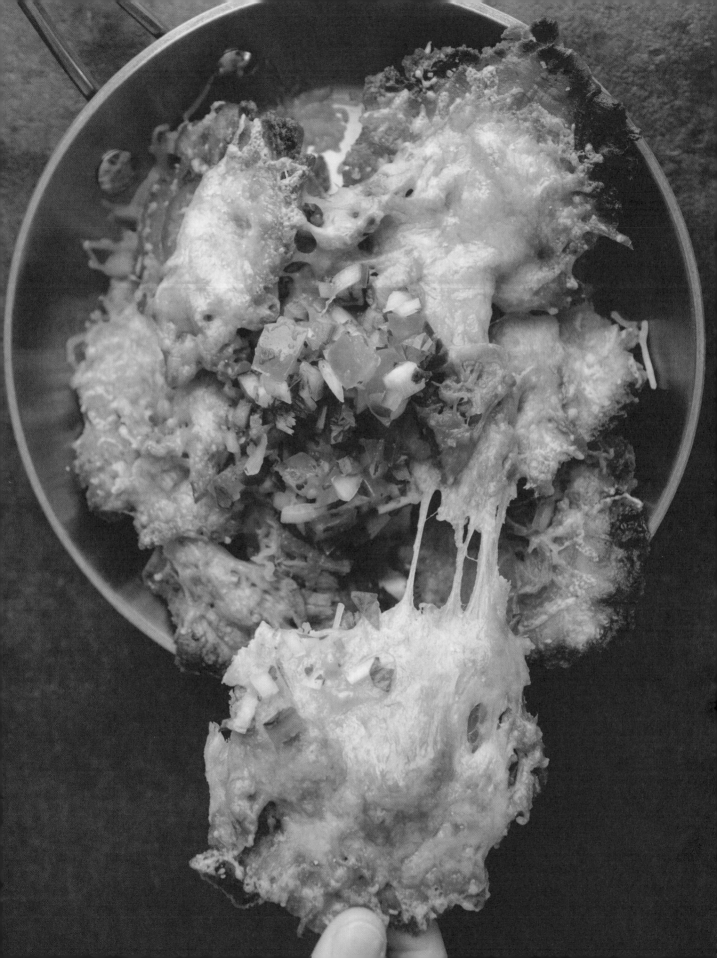

POKÉRITO

MAKES	PREP TIME	COOK TIME	TOTAL TIME
4 burritos	40 minutes	20 minutes	1 hour

Poké is having a moment, and it's great seeing this tasty Hawaiian dish get the attention it deserves. Poké burrito shops have been popping up all over the place, and it's a mash-up I can really get behind.

LIKE THE PROS➡ Using foil to make burritos is a great way to up your burrito-rolling game at home. The foil helps secure everything and will make you feel like you work at a burrito shop.

1. Mix all the poké ingredients and refrigerate until ready to use.

2. Rinse the rice with cold water until the water runs clear.

3. In a small pot, bring rice and 1¾ cups of water to a simmer. Stir, cover, and set the heat to low. Cook for 20 minutes.

4. Remove the rice from the heat, stir, and allow to rest 10 minutes.

5. Transfer the rice to a bowl and add the salt, sugar, and vinegar to taste. Toss for 5 minutes, until the rice cools to room temperature.

6. Peel and pit the avocado, then slice it thin lengthwise.

7. Microwave the tortillas for 20 seconds to soften. Place each onto its own piece of aluminum foil.

8. Layer each tortilla with avocado, rice, poké, cucumber, and carrots.

9. Fold the side of the tortilla closest to you over the top of the fillings and gently squeeze them together to compress. Fold the sides in, and then roll it the rest of the way, making sure to roll it tightly.

10. Wrap the foil around the burrito to secure, and slice it in half.

POKÉ

½ pound bluefin tuna, cut into ½-inch cubes

3 scallions, sliced

1 clove garlic, grated

1 teaspoon red pepper flakes

1 teaspoon sesame seeds

1 tablespoon sesame oil

1 teaspoon rice vinegar

1 teaspoon soy sauce

NACHOS

1 cup sushi rice

1 pinch salt

1 pinch sugar

1 tablespoon rice wine vinegar

WRAP

1 avocado

4 (10- or 12-inch) flour tortillas

1 cup sliced cucumber

1 cup shredded carrots

PHORITO

MAKES	PREP TIME	COOK TIME	TOTAL TIME
4 burritos	15 minutes	15 minutes	30 minutes

My wonderful agent and friend Sally is obsessed with tacos and pho, and her only request for this book was a mash-up of the two. While developing the recipe, I realized that pho is better in burrito form than taco form. The name works better, too. I serve it with beef stock so it becomes almost like a French dip burrito.

GOOD FOR CHEESESTEAKS➡ You can use the shaved beef sold at most grocery stores for this recipe, but Asian markets usually have a sliced beef that's a little thicker than the shaved grocery store kind and works best for this recipe.

1. Bring a pot of water to a boil and remove from the heat. Add the rice noodles and let them soak for about 10 minutes, depending on the brand, until tender. Strain and rinse.

2. In a pot, combine the stock with the ginger, fish sauce, five spice, Sriracha, and hoisin sauce. Bring to a simmer and cook for 5 minutes.

3. Add the beef to the stock and simmer for 5 minutes, until the beef has cooked. Remove the beef from the pot.

4. Meanwhile, microwave the tortillas for 20 seconds to soften. Place each onto its own piece of aluminum foil.

5. Build the burritos by layering the beef, rice noodles, bean sprouts, and basil onto each tortilla.

6. Roll the burrito tight. Fold the side of the tortilla closest to you over the top of the fillings and gently squeeze to compress them. Fold the sides in. Then roll it the rest of the way, making sure that you wrap it tightly. Wrap the foil around the burrito to secure.

7. Serve the burrito with the remaining stock, lime juice, Sriracha, and hoisin sauce.

8 ounces rice noodles

1 quart beef stock

2 inches ginger, grated

2 tablespoons fish sauce

½ teaspoon Chinese five spice

2 tablespoons Sriracha, plus more for serving

1 tablespoon hoisin sauce, plus more for serving

1 pound thin sliced rib eye steak

4 (10- or 12-inch) flour tortillas

2 cups bean sprouts

1 cup Thai basil leaves

fresh lime juice for serving

BURGERS

BURGERITO

MAKES	PREP TIME	COOK TIME	TOTAL TIME
4 burgeritos	10 minutes	35 minutes	45 minutes

I worked at a burrito shop and made this special for my most loyal and favorite customers on my last day of work. It's not a burrito with ground beef, like some cheeseburger burritos out there, but a burrito with an actual burger inside. Caramelized onions in the rice help drive home the burger-burrito mash-up.

1. In a frying pan on medium heat, melt the butter and add the onions. Cook for about 25 minutes, until they brown, stirring often.

2. Mix the rice with the black beans and the browned onions.

3. Mash the avocados and add ¼ cup of the pico de gallo. Stir to combine.

4. Mix the chopped lettuce into the remaining pico de gallo.

5. Form the beef into burger patties and season with the cumin, salt, and pepper.

6. On a grill or in a cast iron pan on high heat, grill the patties to medium doneness, about 5 minutes per side. Melt the cheese on top.

7. Microwave the tortillas for 15 seconds.

8. In each tortilla, layer the rice mixture, a burger, the pico de gallo mixture, and the avocado mixture. Fold the tortilla around the burger, forming more of a sphere than a log. Wrap with foil to seal before serving.

2 tablespoons butter

2 large yellow onions, sliced

2 cups cooked basmati rice

1 cup black beans

2 avocados

1 cup pico de gallo (page 178 or store bought), divided

1 small heart romaine lettuce, chopped

1¼ pounds ground beef

1 tablespoon cumin

salt and pepper

1½ cups Chihuahua cheese

4 (10- or 12-inch) flour tortillas

SCALLION PANCAKE BURGER

MAKES	PREP TIME	COOK TIME	TOTAL TIME
4 burgers	1 hour 30 minutes	10 minutes	1 hour 40 minutes

The Double Awesome—eggs, pesto, and cheese served in a scallion pancake—at Mei Mei in the Back Bay neighborhood of Boston is the best lunch in town, and everyone knows it. I used to live within walking distance of their brick-and-mortar location, and I went there for lunch all the time. After I moved to the other side of town, I was craving this for lunch one day and decided to add a burger to it.

1. Mix the flour with 1 cup of warm water and the salt. Knead for about 10 minutes, until the dough becomes elastic. It should be thick, so add more flour as needed. Wrap with plastic wrap and allow it to rest in the fridge for 30 minutes.

2. Split the dough into 4 pieces and roll them out as thin as possible.

3. Brush the top of the dough with the sesame oil and sprinkle with scallions and jalapeño. Season with salt and pepper.

4. Roll each portion of dough tightly to create a log, then start at one end and form each roll into a coil. Wrap with plastic and let rest an additional 30 minutes.

5. Roll the coils of dough into long flat rectangles.

6. Into a frying pan, pour about ½ inch of vegetable oil and heat it to 350°F.

7. Fry the dough until brown and crispy, about 2 minutes per side.

8. In a food processor, pulse the basil, cilantro, garlic, olive oil, and sesame seeds until they form a chunky pesto.

9. Form patties from the ground beef and, on a grill or in a cast iron pan, cook them on high heat for about 5 minutes per side to medium doneness. Top with the cheese.

10. Cook the eggs over easy.

11. Spread the pesto on half of each scallion pancake. Place the burger on the pesto and top with the egg.

12. Fold the pancake over to form the sandwich.

PANCAKE

2 cups all-purpose flour

½ teaspoon salt

¼ cup sesame oil

1 bunch scallions, finely chopped

1 jalapeño pepper, minced

salt and pepper

vegetable oil for frying

PESTO

1 small bunch basil

1 small bunch cilantro

1 clove garlic

¼ cup olive oil

2 tablespoons sesame seeds

BURGER

1 ¼ pounds ground beef

4 thick slices sharp Cheddar cheese

4 eggs

SPRING ROLL BUN BURGER

MAKES	PREP TIME	COOK TIME	TOTAL TIME
3 large burgers	30 minutes	15 minutes	45 minutes

I ordered a spring roll burger at a restaurant. It contained tiny, bready spring rolls, and they and the bun tasted really dry. When I was re-creating the dish at home, it occurred to me to use the spring rolls as the buns. The barbecue sauce in the giant spring roll buns combined with the homemade sweet and sour sauce on the burger brings all the flavors together.

BIG DIFFERENCE➡ Use spring roll wrappers rather than egg roll wrappers; they're thinner. Asian markets usually carry them in the freezer section.

SWEET & SOUR SAUCE

1. Mix all the sauce ingredients well and set aside.

SPRING ROLLS

2. In a frying pan on high heat, cook the chicken with the vegetable oil, salt, and pepper for about 10 minutes until brown and cooked through. Remove.

3. Add the carrots, cabbage, and scallions and cook on medium heat until softened and reduced in size, about 8 to 10 minutes. Remove.

4. In a large bowl, mix the veggies with the chicken, sambal, and barbecue sauce. Stir well to combine.

5. Form the spring rolls by taking a wrapper, adding some filling, then folding the wrapper over the filling on all sides to form a round bun shape. Wrap the spring roll in a second wrapper, but put the folds on the opposite side this time. Repeat until you have 6 spring roll buns, 2 for each burger.

6. Heat the frying oil to 375°F and fry the rolls for about 3 to 5 minutes. Remove and allow to drain on a rack.

SWEET & SOUR SAUCE

¼ cup honey

2 tablespoons rice vinegar

1 teaspoon chile flakes

1 splash soy sauce

1 splash Sriracha

SPRING ROLLS

½ pound ground chicken

1 tablespoon vegetable oil

salt and pepper

2 cups shredded carrot

2 cups shredded cabbage

1 bunch scallions

2 tablespoons sambal

2 tablespoons barbecue sauce

12 thin spring roll wrappers

canola or peanut oil for frying

BURGERS

1 pound ground beef

3 slices American cheese

1 large tomato, sliced

1 handful baby spinach

BURGERS

7. Form 3 patties from the meat, a little bigger around than the spring rolls. (They'll shrink.)

8. Grill the burgers on high heat for about 5 minutes per side to brown them and cook to a medium doneness. Top with the cheese.

FINISHED DISH

9. Put the first spring roll seam side up on a plate.

10. Top with the burger, tomato, spinach, and Sweet & Sour Sauce.

11. Top with a second spring roll, seam side down, and serve immediately.

THE INGREDIENTS
OF SPRING ROLLS
COMBINED WITH

THE INGREDIENTS
OF A BURGER
MAKE

New
Mash-up!

SPRING ROLL
BUN BURGER

SMOKEHOUSE PAKORA BURGER

MAKES	PREP TIME	COOK TIME	TOTAL TIME
3 big burgers	20 minutes	1 hour 20 minutes	1 hour 40 minutes

If I ever open a food truck or fast-casual restaurant, the theme will be Indian with barbecue flavors. (Good thing I have no desire to open either.) This burger would be the signature dish. It plays on the smokehouse-style burger with onion rings and barbecue sauce that you can find at most places that serve burgers.

IT'S NOT CHEATING→ I've given the long version of the barbecue sauce recipe because it's crazy delicious, but you don't have to go all the way. As a shortcut, mix 1 tablespoon of curry powder and a splash each of vinegar and hot sauce into 1 cup of your favorite store-bought barbecue sauce.

BARBECUE SAUCE

1. Heat a dry frying pan to medium heat and add the cumin, peppercorns, cardamom, coriander, fenugreek, cloves, and cinnamon. Cook for about 3 minutes, until fragrant but not burned.

2. Grind the spices in a spice grinder or with a mortar and pestle. Add the turmeric, paprika, and chile flakes and grind more until combined.

3. Melt the butter over medium heat and cook the onion until fully browned, about 25 minutes. Add the ginger, garlic, and spice mixture and cook for 3 more minutes.

4. Add the can of tomatoes and continue to cook on medium until thick and most of the liquid has evaporated, about 15 more minutes. Add the rest of the ingredients and simmer until thick, about 20 minutes.

5. Using an immersion blender, puree until smooth.

PAKORAS

6. In a bowl, mix the onion, carrots, and jalapeños and add the chickpea flour, garam masala, salt, and cilantro. Stir to combine. Add a splash of warm water and mix. Repeat until the mixture forms a thick batter.

INDIAN BARBECUE SAUCE

1 ½ teaspoons whole cumin

1 teaspoon whole black peppercorns

1 teaspoon whole cardamom

1 teaspoon whole coriander

1 teaspoon whole fenugreek

5 cloves

1 small chunk cinnamon bark

½ teaspoon turmeric

2 teaspoons smoked paprika

1 teaspoon chile flakes

2 tablespoons butter

1 large yellow onion, diced

2 inches ginger, minced

5 cloves garlic, minced

1 (14-ounce) can diced tomatoes

¼ cup molasses

⅓ cup apple cider vinegar

¼ cup agave nectar

¼ cup Worcestershire sauce

3 tablespoons brown sugar

CONTINUED →

PAKORAS

1 white onion, sliced

2 carrots, peeled and julienned

2 jalapeño peppers, julienned

1 cup chickpea flour

1 teaspoon garam masala (page 177 or store bought)

½ teaspoon salt

¼ cup chopped cilantro

canola or peanut oil for frying

BURGERS

1 pound ground beef

salt and pepper

6 (5-inch) rounds naan (page 178 or store bought)

7. Into a frying pan or cast iron skillet, pour 1 inch of oil and heat to 375°F.

8. Spoon clumps of veggie batter, drop gently into the oil, and fry for 5 minutes, until golden and crispy.

9. Remove from the oil and season to taste.

BURGERS

10. Form patties from the ground beef using the naan as a guide for size. Season with salt and pepper.

11. On a grill or cast iron grill pan, brown the burgers on each side on high heat until they reach a medium doneness, about 5 to 7 minutes per side.

12. Place some barbecue sauce onto the bottom naan and top with the burger. Top the burger with more sauce and 2 or 3 pakoras.

13. Top with another piece of naan.

POTATO SKIN BURGER

MAKES	PREP TIME	COOK TIME	TOTAL TIME
5 burgers	30 minutes	1 hour 30 minutes	2 hours

I once made a burger with fries as the bun, but it didn't taste as amazing as I had hoped. When eating potato skins with a friend, I came up with the idea of using potato skins as burger buns. My brain instantly said yes. The trick with skins is that they have a pocket area where the juices of the burger can collect and absorb, whereas the juices run right off a french fry and onto your plate. This recipe also means lots of cheese, bacon, and sour cream.

GROCERY STORE DAYDREAMING ➡ The key to success with this recipe is finding potatoes that are the right size and are clean without many blemishes. Take your time at the store and imagine where you would cut the potato and how bun-like it looks.

5 Yukon Gold potatoes

olive oil

salt and pepper

10 slices bacon

2 cups grated Cheddar cheese

1 pound ground beef (more or less depending on size of potatoes)

1 cup sour cream

½ cup scallions

1. Preheat the oven to 350°F. Rub the potatoes with olive oil and season with salt and pepper.

2. On a lightly oiled baking sheet, bake for 90 minutes, or until tender.

3. Meanwhile, in a large frying pan on medium heat, cook the bacon, flipping occasionally, until browned and crispy, about 5 minutes. Place on a paper towel to cool.

4. Once the bacon has cooled, crumble it and set it aside.

5. Allow the potatoes to cool, then slice them in half to make good-looking buns.

6. Set the oven to 450°F.

7. Place the skins flesh side down on a lightly oiled pan and brush the tops with more oil.

8. Bake for about 10 minutes.

9. Flip the potatoes and fill with cheese and bacon. Return to the oven for 5 minutes, or until the cheese melts.

CONTINUED ➡

10. Meanwhile, form the ground beef into patties, using the buns as your size guide. Season with salt and pepper.

11. On a grill or in a cast iron pan, cook the burgers on high heat for 5 to 7 minutes per side to medium doneness.

12. Fill the skins with sour cream and scallions, then place the between a pair of loaded skins.

THE INGREDIENTS OF <u>POTATO SKINS</u>
COMBINED WITH

THE INGREDIENTS OF A <u>BURGER</u>
MAKE

New Mash-up!

POTATO SKIN BURGER

RAMEN BURGER

MAKES	PREP TIME	COOK TIME	TOTAL TIME
3 burgers	1 hour 20 minutes	20 minutes	1 hour 40 minutes

The ramen burger was huge when it came out and was one of the first mash-ups that excited people about the whole concept of mashing up recipes. Here's my version.

LIKE A SAND CASTLE To mold and press the burger buns, use plastic takeout pints and stack them on top of each other with the noodles pressed between them.

1. Cook the noodles in boiling water until tender. Strain and allow to cool for 3 minutes.

2. Stir in the eggs.

3. Divide the noodles evenly into 6 well-greased containers the size of burger buns and top with 1 more container to make 6 buns. Weigh down the stack so it's tight, firm, and easy to hold. Refrigerate for at least 1 hour or as long as overnight.

4. Mix the hoisin, Sriracha, soy, and ginger to make the sauce.

5. Form burger patties from the ground beef. Make them slightly wider than the buns. Season the burgers aggressively with salt and pepper.

6. Grill or cook the burgers on high heat for about 5 to 7 minutes per side to medium doneness.

7. Unmold the pasta buns and put them in the same pan you used to cook the burgers. Cook them on medium high heat for about 5 minutes per side to firm them up and brown them on both sides.

8. Build the burgers by layering a bun, some arugula, the burger, sauce mixture, and scallions and top with another bun.

8 ounces ramen noodles

2 eggs, slightly beaten

¼ cup hoisin sauce

1 tablespoon Sriracha

1 tablespoon soy sauce

1 teaspoon grated ginger

1 pound ground beef

salt and pepper

1 cup baby arugula

½ cup chopped scallions

THE INGREDIENTS OF RAMEN COMBINED WITH ➡

THE INGREDIENTS OF A BURGER MAKE ➡

New Mash-up! RAMEN BURGER

STROGANOFF BURGER

MAKES	PREP TIME	COOK TIME	TOTAL TIME
3 burgers	1 hour 20 minutes	20 minutes	1 hour 40 minutes

After the Ramen Burger, I thought it would be fun to make another pasta-bun burger. This one was a top choice because a burger with a mushroom and cream sauce just seems so right. The pasta sticks together really well, so it won't fall apart, and the creamy sauce brings it all together.

8 ounces egg noodles

2 eggs

1 large yellow onion, sliced

1 tablespoon butter

4 ounces mushrooms, sliced

¼ cup cream

½ cup sour cream

1 pound ground beef

salt and pepper

1. Cook the egg noodles in boiling water until tender, about 6–8 minutes, depending on the brand. Strain and allow to cool for 3 minutes.

2. Whisk in the eggs.

3. Divide noodles evenly into 6 well-greased containers the size of burger buns and top with 1 more container to make 6 buns. Weigh down the stack so it's tight, firm, and easy to hold. Refrigerate for at least 1 hour or as long as overnight.

4. Cook the onion in the butter on medium heat until it browns, about 15 minutes.

5. Add the mushrooms and cook for 5 minutes. Add the cream and stir to coat.

6. Remove from the heat. Add the sour cream and stir to combine.

7. Form burger patties from the ground beef. Make them slightly wider than the buns. Season the burgers aggressively with salt and pepper.

8. Grill or cook the burgers on high heat for about 5 to 7 minutes per side to medium doneness.

9. Unmold the pasta buns and put them in the same pan you used to cook the burgers. Cook them on medium-high heat for about 5 minutes per side to firm them up and brown them on both sides.

10. Build the burgers by layering a noodle bun, the burger patty, mushroom cream sauce, and another noodle bun.

S'MORES BURGER

MAKES	PREP TIME	COOK TIME	TOTAL TIME
9 large sliders	15 minutes	10 minutes	25 minutes

At a recent grilling party, someone broke into the s'mores a little prematurely. In my line of sight, the marshmallow was browning directly in front of a burger on the grill, and the gooey browned marshmallow looked just like cheese on the burger. I pulled out my phone and thumbed a quick note to myself: MAKE S'MORES BURGERS IMMEDIATELY. Marshmallow, chocolate, and graham are one of the best flavor combinations in the world, and it's no secret that chocolate and caramel go great with a bit of salt.

FIND A STICK➡ Instead of using store-bought marshmallow creme and a broiler, you can use large marshmallows and toast them as you grill the burger. Put them on top of the finished burger and smash it down with the top bun. Also, watch out for molten chocolate when biting into this thing!

1 pound ground beef

5 ounces dark chocolate

salt

2 cups marshmallow creme

10 graham crackers, broken in half to form 20 squares

10 small burger buns

1. Divide the beef into nine small patties.

2. Break the chocolate into single squares so they can lie in a single layer in the center of the patties, about ½ ounce of chocolate per burger.

3. Wrap the meat around the chocolate and make the burgers about the same size as the graham cracker squares. Salt well.

4. Grill each burger on one side for about 5 minutes.

5. Flip it and top with marshmallow creme. Brown the top of the marshmallow either under a broiler or with a kitchen blowtorch.

6. Meanwhile, lightly toast the buns.

7. To make the sliders, place a graham cracker square on the bottom bun. Top with the burger, another cracker, and the top bun.

MAIN DISHES

BUFFALO CHICKEN PAD THAI

MAKES	PREP TIME	COOK TIME	TOTAL TIME
4 servings	30 minutes	30 minutes	1 hour

The idea for this tasty abomination came to me, after many beers, when I was raiding the fridge late on a Saturday night. I put some left-over boneless Buffalo wings into leftover pad Thai. Thankfully, I had the wherewithal to write down how truly awesome this experience tasted and made a more thoughtful version of it a few days later.

1. Cook the noodles according to package instructions. Set aside.

2. Combine all the sauce ingredients.

3. Bread the chicken: Fill three bowls with the flour, eggs, and panko, respectively. Heat a thin layer of oil in a frying pan. Slice the chicken into nugget-sized chunks, cutting the breasts across the short direction.

4. Salt the nuggets to taste, then dredge them in the flour, then the eggs, then the panko.

5. Pan-fry the chicken on medium-high heat for 10 minutes, until browned, flipping once halfway through cooking. Slice the nuggets into bite-sized strips.

6. In a frying pan with some vegetable oil, cook the carrots and celery on high heat for about 5 minutes. Add the ginger and garlic and cook for 2 minutes. Add the scallions and stir to combine.

7. Spread the veggies around the edges of the pan. Pour the eggs into the center and scramble. Cook for 5 minutes, continuing to scramble.

8. Add the noodles to the pan and stir to combine everything.

9. Pour the noodles onto a serving dish. Top with the chicken strips and serve with additional carrots and celery.

12 ounces flat rice noodles

SAUCE

½ cup cayenne hot sauce

¼ cup fish sauce

¼ cup rice vinegar

juice of 3 limes

2 tablespoons sugar

CHICKEN

1 cup all-purpose flour

2 eggs, beaten

1 cup panko bread crumbs

vegetable oil

2 chicken breasts

salt

4 carrots, peeled and julienned, plus 1 for garnish

4 celery sticks, julienned, plus 1 for garnish

2 tablespoons grated ginger

3 cloves garlic, grated

7 scallions, chopped

3 eggs, beaten

BIBIMBAP RICE TARTS

MAKES	PREP TIME	COOK TIME	TOTAL TIME
6 tarts	30 minutes	45 minutes	1 hour 15 minutes

Once I made a rice tart, I realized that it could be a great way to serve bibimbap. The best bibimbap comes in a stone bowl called a *dolsot*, and the bottom of the rice gets crispy (which the Spanish call *socarrat* in paella). Baking the rice in a tart shape can give you that nice, crispy rice texture as well.

1. Mix the beef with the soy sauce, pear, scallions, garlic, ginger, and sugar. Allow to marinate for 30 minutes.

2. Mix the rice with 3 cups of water and bring to a simmer. Reduce the heat and cover. Cook for 20 minutes, until the rice becomes tender. Remove from the heat and let sit for 10 minutes.

3. Stir the rice with the sesame oil and salt to taste and toss for about 8 minutes, until it cools. Try doing this in front of a fan or outside in cold weather.

4. Preheat the oven to 450°F.

5. Butter 6 small tart pans or mini springform pans. Divide the rice into each of these, forming a little bowl of rice inside each pan.

6. Bake the rice for 20 minutes, until the edges crisp a little.

7. Meanwhile, in about 1 tablespoon of sesame oil, sauté the mushrooms, zucchini, carrots, and spinach on high heat for about 3 to 5 minutes each, one at a time, removing each to a paper towel as you go. Add more sesame oil if needed.

8. In the same pan, cook the eggs, sunny side up; remove when done.

9. In the same pan, cook the meat on high heat for about 5 minutes.

10. Unmold the rice tarts. Carefully place an egg into the center of each rice tart, then put the veggies and meat around the egg yolk, alternating them in a decorative circle.

11. Garnish with a drizzle of Sriracha.

½ pound rib eye steak, thinly sliced

¼ cup soy sauce

1 pear, grated with juices

2 scallions, sliced

1 clove garlic, grated

1 inch ginger, grated

1 teaspoon brown sugar

2 cups sushi rice

2 tablespoons sesame oil, plus more for sautéing

salt

butter for greasing

5 ounces mushrooms, sliced

1 zucchini, julienned

3 carrots, shredded

8 ounces chopped baby spinach

6 eggs

Sriracha for garnish

RICE & BEAN TART

MAKES	PREP TIME	COOK TIME	TOTAL TIME
6 servings	30 minutes	30 minutes	1 hour

Sticky sushi rice inspired me to use rice as crust. A tart seemed like a good idea because, if the rice stays together enough, you can eat it like a pizza. The dish starts with a classic rice-and-beans profile, but chorizo fat in the beans pushes it over the edge.

1. Add the sushi rice to a pot with 3 cups of water. Bring to a simmer, cover, and reduce the heat to low. Cook for 20 minutes. Remove from the heat and allow to sit for 10 minutes.

2. In a bowl, mix the red wine vinegar, paprika, sugar, turmeric, and salt. Add the cooked rice and toss for about 8 minutes, until it cools. Try doing this in front of a fan or outside in cold weather.

3. Preheat the oven to 375°F.

4. Grease a tart pan with butter and spread the rice thinly in it, forming a crust.

5. Cook the chorizo on high heat for about 3 minutes, until it browns. Remove from the pan but keep the fat in the pan.

6. Add the onion to the chorizo fat and cook on medium-high for 5 minutes, then add the beans. Mash the onions and beans while they cook, stirring and mashing until everything combines. Remove from the heat.

7. Spread the beans onto the rice crust. Top with the chorizo, followed by the diced tomatoes.

8. Top with cheese and bake for 30 to 40 minutes.

9. Remove from the oven and allow to rest for 5 minutes before removing it from the tart pan.

2 cups sushi rice

3 tablespoons red wine vinegar

1 teaspoon paprika

1 teaspoon sugar

½ teaspoon turmeric

1 pinch salt

butter for greasing

½ pound chorizo, chopped into quarter rounds

1 small yellow onion, diced

2 (15-ounce) cans black beans, strained and rinsed

1 (14-ounce) can diced tomatoes

1 cup shredded Cheddar cheese

CRAB RANGOON MAC & CHEESE

MAKES	PREP TIME	COOK TIME	TOTAL TIME
4 servings	20 minutes	25 minutes	45 minutes

Crab rangoon is my favorite late-night drunk food. Many years ago, my roommate and I ordered it every Saturday at 3 a.m., and it was the highlight of our week. Rangoons are basically fried wontons filled with cream cheese, and they don't contain much if any crab. This crab rangoon–inspired mac and cheese has lots of real crab in it.

½ pound macaroni

½ pound lump crab

8 ounces cream cheese

8 ounces Monterey Jack cheese, shredded

2 tablespoons soy sauce

¼ cup whole milk

1 bunch scallions, chopped

½ cup pickled jalapeño peppers, sliced or chopped (optional)

½ tablespoon red chile flakes

12 wonton wrappers

1 tablespoon vegetable oil

salt

1. Preheat the oven to 350°F.

2. Cook the pasta al dente, according to the package directions. Reserve ½ cup of the pasta water, drain the rest, and set the cooked pasta aside.

3. In a bowl, mix the crab, cheeses, soy sauce, milk, scallions, jalapeños, and chile flakes. Stir well.

4. Add the reserved pasta water to the cheese mixture and stir well.

5. Add the pasta to the cheese mixture and stir.

6. Place in a 1-quart baking dish or divide between 4 (8-ounce) ramekins. Bake for 25 to 30 minutes, until bubbly and creamy.

7. While the pasta is baking, cut the wonton wrappers into triangles.

8. Heat the vegetable oil in a skillet and fry the wonton pieces in batches, until crisp. Drain and season with salt to taste.

9. Serve the pasta with the wonton wrappers on the side.

 THE INGREDIENTS OF CRAB RANGOON COMBINED WITH ➡

 THE INGREDIENTS OF MAC & CHEESE MAKE ➡

 New Mash-up! CRAB RANGOON MAC & CHEESE

CARNITAS BURRITO CABBAGE ROLLS

MAKES	PREP TIME	COOK TIME	TOTAL TIME
8 rolls	45 minutes	30 minutes	1 hour 15 minutes

I used to run a burrito shop, and all I thought about was burritos: filling ideas, working the flavors into different dishes, and, as in this dish, alternate wraps for burrito ingredients. Recipes for cabbage rolls often feature meat, rice, and tomatoes, so these dishes blend very naturally.

PATIENCE MAKES PERFECT➡ Peeling cabbage leaves without breaking them can be the toughest part of this recipe, but with a little patience it isn't that hard. Some people like to peel the vegetable and then boil it, but I find it easier to peel the leaves when they're softer.

1 head cabbage

1 cup pico de gallo (page 178 or store bought)

1 (14-ounce) can diced tomatoes

2 cups cooked white basmati rice

1 (15-ounce) can black beans, strained and rinsed

2 cups carnitas (page 176 or store bought)

2 cups grated Cheddar cheese

guacamole for serving

sour cream for serving

1. Bring a large pot of water to a boil and drop in the head of cabbage. Simmer about 20 minutes to soften.

2. Peel off 8 large leaves. Use a paring knife to cut the giant stem off the bottom of each leaf.

3. Pour the pico de gallo and the tomatoes into the bottom of a baking dish that will snugly fit all 8 cabbage rolls.

4. Preheat the oven to 350°F.

5. Place about ¼ cup of rice into a cabbage leaf, then ¼ cup carnitas and a few tablespoons of black beans.

6. Starting at the stem end, roll the cabbage leaf halfway, then fold in the sides and roll the rest of the way.

7. Place the roll into the baking dish, nestling it into the sauce.

8. Repeat with the remaining rolls. Top with the cheese.

9. Bake for 30 minutes.

10. To serve, scoop the rolls onto a plate with plenty of the sauce from the bottom of the pan. Top with guacamole and sour cream.

CHICKEN PARM TIKKA MASALA

MAKES	PREP TIME	COOK TIME	TOTAL TIME
4 to 6 servings	45 minutes	45 minutes	1 hour 30 minutes

Chicken tikka masala is a great entry-level dish for people who think they don't like Indian food. It's also one of the original mash-ups, made in the UK to warm British palates to Indian cuisine. If you need to go one step further to convince a stubborn eater to try Indian, you can't go wrong with this combo of tikka masala and chicken parm. At this point, it shouldn't surprise you how well Indian and Italian flavors go together, but this dish will remind you how delicious the combination tastes.

SAUCE

1. In a medium-sized heavy-bottomed pot, add the onion and butter. Season with salt and pepper. Cook on medium heat for about 15 minutes, until the onions brown around the edges.

2. Add the garlic and ginger and cook for 3 minutes. Add the curry powder and chile flakes and cook for 2 minutes.

3. Add the crushed tomatoes, diced tomatoes, honey, and cream and simmer for about 45 minutes.

CHICKEN

4. Preheat the oven to 450°F.

5. Fill three bowls respectively with the flour mixed with salt and pepper to taste, the egg, and the breadcrumbs mixed with 1 cup of the paneer cheese.

6. Dredge each cutlet in the flour. Shake off the excess flour and coat with the eggs. Let the excess liquid drip off and then coat in the breadcrumb mixture. Press the breadcrumbs to bind to the chicken firmly. Repeat with the rest of the cutlets.

7. In a large frying pan, cook the chicken on medium-high heat in batches in about ¼ inch oil to brown on both sides, about 3 to 5 minutes per side.

SAUCE

1 large yellow onion

2 tablespoons butter

salt and pepper

5 cloves garlic, grated

2 inches ginger, grated

2 tablespoons curry powder (page 176 or store bought)

1 tablespoon chile flakes

1 (28-ounce) can crushed tomatoes

1 (28-ounce) can diced tomatoes

2 tablespoons honey

1 cup cream

CHICKEN

1 cup all-purpose flour

salt and pepper

2 eggs, beaten

1 cup plain breadcrumbs

2 cups paneer cheese, crumbled, divided

1½ pounds chicken breast cutlets

olive oil for browning

3 cups cooked white basmati rice

cilantro for garnish

8. Place the cutlets on a baking sheet and repeat until you've browned all of the chicken.

9. Top each cutlet with a spoonful of sauce and a sprinkle of the remaining paneer cheese. Bake for 10 minutes.

10. Meanwhile, add ½ cup of sauce to the rice and stir to combine.

11. Serve by layering the rice, a spoonful of sauce, then a piece of chicken. Garnish with cilantro.

THE INGREDIENTS OF
CHICKEN PARMESAN
COMBINED WITH

THE INGREDIENTS OF
CHICKEN TIKKA MASALA
MAKE

New
Mash-up!

CHICKEN PARM

TIKKA MASALA

CHILI RISOTTO

MAKES	PREP TIME	COOK TIME	TOTAL TIME
6 servings	1 hour 30 minutes	40 minutes	2 hours 10 minutes

Some recipes call for reconstituting dried chile peppers in water but then discarding the chile water. That seemed like a waste because a lot of the flavor from the chiles ends up in that water. I brainstormed for a bit on how to use that water, and I came up with this recipe.

1. Bring the chicken stock to a simmer.

2. Remove the stems and seeds from the chile peppers and add half of them to a frying pan on medium heat. Cook for about 3 minutes, while stirring. Be aware that this will make the air in your kitchen hard to breathe.

3. Add the chiles to the simmering stock and repeat with the remaining chiles.

4. Remove the stock from the heat and allow to steep for 1 hour.

5. Use a stick or countertop blender to blend the stock and chiles until smooth.

6. In a large heavy-bottomed pot, cook the ground beef with some olive oil on high heat to brown, about 7 minutes. Remove from the pot.

7. Add the onion, bell pepper, and jalapeños and cook on high heat about 10 minutes to brown the edges of the veggies lightly.

8. Add the rice and cook for 3 minutes, allowing the oil to coat the grains of rice. Add more oil if needed.

9. Add the garlic and cook for 3 more minutes. Add the beef back to the pot.

10. Add the beer and stir well, scraping the bottom of the pan to get all the browned bits off the pot and into the risotto. Reduce the heat to medium-low.

1 quart chicken stock

5 ancho chile peppers

5 guajillo chile peppers

5 New Mexico chile peppers

1 pound ground beef

olive oil for browning

1 white onion, diced

1 green bell pepper, diced

5 jalapeño peppers, seeds removed and diced

1 cup Arborio rice

3 cloves garlic, minced

1 (12-ounce) can IPA beer

1 (28-ounce) can diced tomatoes

1 (14-ounce) can black beans, strained and rinsed

2 tablespoons honey

1 tablespoon cumin

½ tablespoon chipotle powder

½ tablespoon Mexican oregano

sour cream for serving

scallions for serving

cilantro for serving

THE INGREDIENTS
OF <u>CHILI</u>
COMBINED WITH

↓

THE INGREDIENTS
OF <u>RISOTTO</u>
MAKE

↓

New
Mash-up!

CHILI RISOTTO

11. Cook for about 5 minutes, stirring, until the beer has evaporated a bit. Add the tomatoes, beans, honey, cumin, chipotle, and oregano. Cook another 5 minutes.

12. Add 1 ladleful of the stock mixture, stir well, and continue to cook and stir. Add another ladleful of stock every time the liquid level gets low.

13. Cook until the rice is tender, about 30 minutes. The risotto mixture should look loose and soupy rather than tight and dry. If you run out of stock before the rice is tender, you can add water. Serve with sour cream, scallions, and cilantro.

CUBANO MAC & CHEESE LASAGNA

MAKES	PREP TIME	COOK TIME	TOTAL TIME
8 servings	45 minutes	45 minutes	1 hour 30 minutes

This dish has a lot going on. If you think about it, it's a *triple* mash-up. You need lasagna noodles instead of normal pasta elbows because the shape of the dish emulates a pressed sandwich.

1. In a frying pan, cook the pork on high heat with some oil, salt, and pepper. Remove from the heat when nicely brown and cooked through, about 10 minutes.

2. In a large heavy-bottomed pot, melt the butter. Add the onions and sweat them on medium-high heat for about 5 minutes.

3. Add the flour and whisk until it combines well with the butter. Keep stirring for about 3 minutes until the color changes to a golden hue.

4. Whisk in the milk, making sure to eliminate all the lumps. Bring to a boil, at which point the roux will cause it to thicken instantly. Reduce the heat to low and allow to cool for 5 minutes.

5. Add the cheeses to the pot in small batches, letting each batch melt before you add more.

6. Add the mustard and pickle juice.

7. Preheat the oven to 350°F.

8. Cook the noodles in salted boiling water for 7 minutes. You want to undercook them because they will cook more in the sauce.

9. Build the lasagna by layering sauce, noodles, ham, pickles, and pork. Repeat to fill the pan.

10. Bake uncovered for 45 minutes. The top should brown nicely, but if it doesn't, give it a few minutes under the broiler. Let it rest for about 20 minutes before cutting and serving.

1 pound boneless country pork ribs, diced

olive oil

salt and pepper

4 tablespoons butter

1 small yellow onion, diced

¼ cup all-purpose flour

3 cups whole milk

8 ounces Cheddar cheese, grated

8 ounces Gruyère cheese, grated

8 ounces Monterey Jack cheese, grated

8 ounces Swiss cheese, grated

⅓ cup yellow mustard

1 cup dill pickle juice

1 pound lasagna noodles

½ pound sliced rosemary ham

4 or 5 medium dill pickles, sliced thin

EVERYTHING BAGEL MAC & CHEESE

MAKES	PREP TIME	COOK TIME	TOTAL TIME
8 servings	20 minutes	1 hour 15 minutes	1 hour 35 minutes

The cream cheese sauce makes this a perfect flavor mash-up of an everything bagel and mac and cheese. But the homemade everything spice tastes amazing. Letting onion and garlic essentially dehydrate in your oven for an hour or so really intensifies the flavors.

1. Preheat the oven to 350°F.

2. On a large baking sheet, mix the onions and garlic with the olive oil and salt.

3. Bake, stirring occasionally, for about 1 hour, until brown and crispy.

4. When just about browned, mix in the poppy and sesame seeds, and cook another 5 to 10 minutes to toast them lightly.

5. Mix together the cream, cream cheese, Fontina, Monterey Jack, and scallions.

6. Boil some salted water and cook the pasta. When the pasta has 3 minutes of cooking time left, pour ½ cup of the pasta water into the cheese mixture. Mix well so the cheeses to melt.

7. Strain the pasta, add it to the cheese, and mix well. By now, the cheeses should have melted and formed a sauce.

8. Pour into a baking dish and mix in the onion and garlic spice mixture. You may not want to use all of it, so use discretion and taste.

9. Set the oven to 450°F.

10. Toast the bagels. In a food processor, pulse them to crumbs.

11. Sprinkle the bagel crumbs on the pasta. Bake for about 15 minutes, until bubbly and brown.

2 yellow onions, diced

3 cloves garlic, diced

1 teaspoon olive oil

1 pinch salt

1 ½ tablespoons poppy seeds

1 ½ tablespoons sesame seeds

1 cup cream

12 ounces cream cheese

8 ounces Fontina cheese

8 ounces shredded Monterey Jack cheese

12 scallions, chopped

1 pound macaroni

2 everything bagels, sliced into thin horizontal rounds

GNOCCHI GOBI

MAKES	PREP TIME	COOK TIME	TOTAL TIME
6 servings	1 hour	1 hour 30 minutes	2 hours 30 minutes

Gnocchi have subbed for other forms of potato many times in my recipes, and a few of those recipes appear in this book. This dish uses gnocchi in aloo gobi, the iconic Indian dish starring potatoes and cauliflower. In this twist, the gnocchi join cauliflower and peas in a spicy tomato curry.

1. Prepare the gnocchi according to page 177 or the package directions.

2. Preheat the oven to 500°F.

3. Break the head of cauliflower into uniformly small pieces, about the same size as the gnocchi (bite-size). Toss in a splash of olive oil and salt and spread the pieces on a baking sheet.

4. Roast for about 10 minutes, until they brown and cook through.

5. Sauté the onion in the butter on medium heat until very brown, about 20 minutes.

6. Add the garlic, ginger, and curry powder and mix well. Cook for about 2 minutes, then add the tomatoes.

7. Stir well and scrape the bottom of the pan to release any stuck food. Add the peas and simmer for 5 minutes.

8. Boil the gnocchi for about 5 minutes, until they float and have cooked fully. Strain and gently toss the gnocchi and the cauliflower with the sauce. Garnish with cilantro.

12 ounces fresh gnocchi (page 177 or store bought)

1 head cauliflower

1 tablespoon olive oil

1 yellow onion, sliced

2 tablespoons butter

3 cloves garlic, minced

2 tablespoons minced ginger

1 tablespoon curry powder (page 176 or store bought)

1 (28-ounce) can diced tomatoes

1 cup peas, fresh or frozen

cilantro for garnish

THE INGREDIENTS OF GNOCCHI COMBINED WITH ➡

THE INGREDIENTS OF ALOO GOBI MAKE ➡

New Mash-up!   GNOCCHI GOBI

LOADED GNOCCHI

MAKES	PREP TIME	COOK TIME	TOTAL TIME
4 bowls	40 minutes	15 minutes	55 minutes

This recipe, which continues the theme of gnocchi in place of potatoes, was the first time I used this technique, and its success spurred the rest of the ideas. The school cafeteria at my elementary school had a baked potato bar, and I loved loading chili onto my potatoes. When I do loaded potato recipes now, chili immediately comes to mind, but you can make these gnocchi with whatever you like putting on your baked potatoes.

CHILI STYLES➡ The chili in this recipe is thick and meaty, with no beans and only a few veggies cooked down so much they almost melt in the sauce. It has more of a sloppy Joe texture—the kind you'll find on a Coney Island hot dog. Feel free to swap it out for your favorite chili recipe or store bought.

CHILI

1. In a pot or large frying pan, cook the beef, onion, and jalapeños on high heat with the oil. Season with salt and pepper and cook for about 20 minutes to brown the meat and veggies lightly.

2. Add the garlic and cook for 2 minutes. Add the cumin, paprika, chili powder, oregano, coriander, and cinnamon. Stir and cook for 3 minutes.

3. Add the tomatoes and sugar and stir to combine. Season with more salt and pepper. Cook for about 20 minutes to reduce and thicken.

GNOCCHI

4. Bring a pot of salted water to a boil and drop in the gnocchi for about 5 minutes.

5. In a large frying pan, melt the butter. Strain the gnocchi and add them to the butter. Stir to coat.

6. Remove from the heat, add the sour cream, and stir to combine.

7. Divide the gnocchi into four bowls and top with the chili, scallions, and cheese.

CHILI

1 pound ground beef

1 small yellow onion, diced

3 jalapeño peppers, diced and seeds removed

1 tablespoon olive oil

salt and pepper

2 cloves garlic, minced

1 tablespoon cumin

½ tablespoon smoked paprika

½ tablespoon chili powder

2 teaspoons oregano

½ teaspoon coriander

¼ teaspoon cinnamon

1 (28-ounce) can petite diced tomatoes with juices

1 teaspoon sugar

CHILI

1 pound gnocchi (page 177 or store bought)

4 tablespoons butter

1 cup sour cream

1 bunch scallions, chopped

1 cup grated Cheddar cheese

MAPO TOFU BOLOGNESE

MAKES	PREP TIME	COOK TIME	TOTAL TIME
4 to 6 servings	30 minutes	1 hour	1 hour 30 minutes

One day, while enjoying some mapo tofu, I realized that it reminded me of a meaty pasta sauce. The inspiration for this recipe was that simple. I worked on the recipe, adding some noodles and tomatoes to evoke a Bolognese sauce, and it came out amazing.

HOMEMADE VS. STORE BOUGHT➡ I don't consider fresh pasta any better than dried. I've used both when making this dish, so it's totally up to you how you want to approach this dish. There are lots of great options for dried noodles and places where you can buy fresh noodles instead of making them yourself. Either way, this sauce deserves something special, so if you do use dried, find a unique cut or brand that you don't use every day.

1 tablespoon vegetable oil, plus more as needed

1 pound ground beef

1 tablespoon Sichuan peppercorns

½ cup diced yellow onion

½ cup diced carrot

½ cup diced celery

½ cup diced cabbage

3 cloves garlic, minced

1 inch ginger, minced

5 red Thai chiles, sliced, plus more for garnish

1 teaspooon Sichuan peppercorns, ground

2 tablespoons soy sauce

2 tablespoons fermented bean paste

¼ cup Xiaoxing wine

1 (14-ounce) can diced tomatoes

2 cups chicken stock

7 ounces tofu, diced

1 pound tagliatelle or other thick noodles

scallions for garnish

1. In a large heavy-bottomed pan, add the vegetable oil and the beef and sear on high heat to brown and cook it through, about 8 minutes, making sure to get good color on the meat. Remove from the pan.

2. Add the whole Sichuan peppercorns and a little extra oil if needed. Cook on medium heat for about 2 minutes to brown the peppercorns and infuse the oil. Remove the peppercorns from the pot but retain the oil.

3. Add the onion, carrot, celery, and cabbage and cook on medium-high heat for about 10 minutes, until lightly starting to brown.

4. Add the garlic, ginger, and chiles and cook for 3 more minutes.

5. Add the ground peppercorns and stir to combine.

6. Add the soy sauce, bean paste, and wine and cook for 5 more minutes, stirring often.

7. Add the tomatoes and cook for another 5 minutes, stirring often.

8. Add the chicken stock. Lower the heat to a light simmer and let the mixture reduce and thicken for about 45 minutes.

9. After the meat mixture has reduced and thickened, add the tofu and stir well. The tofu should crumble into small balls.

10. Meanwhile, bring a pot of salted water to a boil.

11. Drop in the pasta and cook until al dente.

12. Transfer the pasta into the sauce along with ¼ cup of the pasta water and stir well.

13. Top with scallions and chiles.

GENERAL TSO'S CHICKEN & PORK FRIED RICE WAFFLES

MAKES	PREP TIME	COOK TIME	TOTAL TIME
4 servings	45 minutes	30 minutes	1 hour 15 minutes

Seeing someone put leftover fried rice into a waffle maker to heat it up immediately gave me this idea. Instead of just putting plain rice in the waffle iron and topping it with your standard General Tso's chicken, I decided to blend the two dishes. I mixed the rice into waffle batter and added maple syrup to the spicy sour sauce. Pouring that sauce over chicken and waffles makes this dish look more like classic chicken and waffles, but it tastes more like General Tso. Fun!

WAFFLE MAKER HACK➡ For best success, anything you put into a waffle iron should be room temperature or warmer. Otherwise, it will cool the iron too much to function properly. If your waffle mixture is too cold, microwave it for a few seconds, stirring and repeating in small increments until it has warmed a bit.

WAFFLES

1. In a large bowl, mix the rice, soy sauce, wine, sesame oil, vinegar, pork, scallions, chiles, and eggs.

2. Stir the flour and baking powder together and then stir them into the bowl with the rice. Stir well. You want a thick batter for this mixture.

3. Preheat the waffle iron. Preheat the oven to 200°F.

4. Cook the batter in batches in the iron according to the manufacturer's instructions.

5. Put the cooked waffles on a baking sheet and place into the oven to stay hot until ready to use.

CHICKEN

6. Cut the chicken into nugget-sized pieces, using the shape of the thighs to dictate where to make the cuts. Cut along the creases and fat pockets.

RICE WAFFLES

1½ cups cooked white rice

2 tablespoons soy sauce

1 tablespoon Shaoxing rice wine

½ tablespoon sesame oil

½ tablespoon rice wine vinegar

½ cup cooked pork, chopped finely

5 scallions, chopped into small rounds

3 red Thai chile peppers, seeds removed and diced

2 eggs

½ cup all-purpose flour

1 teaspoon baking powder

CHICKEN

1½ pounds boneless skinless chicken thighs

2 tablespoons soy sauce

1 egg

salt

½ cup all-purpose flour

½ cup cornstarch

½ teaspoon baking powder

canola or peanut oil for frying

CONTINUED ➡

7. In a mixing bowl, toss the chicken with the soy sauce and egg. Lightly salt.

8. In a large bowl, mix the flour, cornstarch, and baking powder.

9. Add some of the flour mixture to the chicken, stirring and adding a little more, until you coat the chicken in a thick mixture of clumpy flour.

10. Preheat the oil to 375°F.

11. Fry the chicken in batches, about 5 minutes per batch, until they lightly brown and cook through.

FINISHED DISH

12. Stir all the sauce ingredients together.

13. Top each waffle with a few pieces of chicken and pour plenty of the sauce on top of the whole dish.

SAUCE

¼ cup sambal chile paste

¼ cup maple syrup

¼ cup honey

2 tablespoons soy sauce

1 tablespoon rice vinegar

1 tablespoon sesame oil

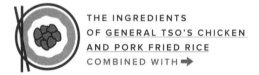

THE INGREDIENTS OF GENERAL TSO'S CHICKEN AND PORK FRIED RICE COMBINED WITH ➡

THE INGREDIENTS OF WAFFLES MAKE ➡

New Mash-up!

GENERAL TSO'S CHICKEN & PORK FRIED RICE WAFFLES

SPINACH & ARTICHOKE GNUDI

MAKES	PREP TIME	COOK TIME	TOTAL TIME
4 servings	20 minutes	20 minutes	40 minutes

Gnudi are ravioli without clothes. Skip the pasta and get right to the filling. Most versions have spinach and ricotta, which reminded me of the classic spinach and artichoke dip that was so popular at restaurants in the 1990s and 2000s. I added a little semolina flour to the dip recipe and boiled it, and these gnudi were born.

PRO-TIP➡ Pita chips as breadcrumbs take this mash-up to the next level. When creating mash-ups of your own, think creatively about how to repurpose everything from each source dish.

1. In a large bowl, mix all the gnudi ingredients. Allow to rest in the fridge for 30 minutes.

2. Form small balls—about the size of large gnocchi—from the gnudi mixture. Roll each ball in semolina flour. Place on a baking sheet lined with parchment paper and cover lightly with plastic wrap.

3. In a food processor, pulse the pita chips until they are the size of large breadcrumbs.

4. Bring a large pot of water to a boil.

5. In a large frying pan, melt the butter. Add the onion and cook on medium heat for about 15 minutes, until the onion softens and starts to brown.

6. Add the garlic and cook for 2 minutes.

7. Stir in the cream and simmer for 5 minutes.

8. Drop the gnudi into the boiling water and cook for about 5 minutes, until they float.

9. Strain out the gnudi and add them to the sauce.

10. Remove from the heat and stir in the Parmesan cheese and parsley.

11. Top with the pita chip crumbs.

GNUDI

1 cup ricotta cheese

½ cup chopped frozen spinach, drained and squeezed dry

½ cup diced marinated artichokes

½ cup grated Parmesan cheese

2 eggs

1 pinch freshly grated nutmeg

¼ cup semolina flour, plus more for coating

salt and pepper

SAUCE AND GARNISH

10 or so pita chips (enough for 1 cup of crumbs)

1 tablespoon butter

1 small yellow onion, diced

1 clove garlic, minced

½ cup cream

½ cup grated Parmesan cheese

¼ cup chopped parsley

BARBECUE CHICKEN PIZZA CAKE

MAKES	PREP TIME	COOK TIME	TOTAL TIME
1 large pizza cake, 4 to 6 servings	45 minutes	45 minutes	1 hour 30 minutes

Like so many viral recipes, the pizza cake craze that hit the Internet a few years ago looked better than it tasted. The few versions that I tried somehow came out dry yet soggy at the same time. I decided to treat it as more of a calzone than a pizza and really load up the toppings. That's when it started getting interesting. My favorite calzone filling, barbecue chicken, makes this the pizza cake I've been craving.

LOGISTICAL ISSUES➡ The pan is just as important as the rest of the recipe. My favorite way to cook it is in an empty #10 can with the top and bottom removed. This also helps because, to remove the pizza from the can, you need only lift off the can. I also have done this in a 6-inch-deep cake pan that had heavy-duty foil reinforcing the sides to extend the depth to 8 inches. The foil on the side will help you remove the cake from the pan as well.

1 pound boneless skinless chicken thighs

1 red onion, half diced and half sliced thin

1 tablespoon vegetable oil, plus more for greasing

¼ cup rice vinegar

½ cup barbecue sauce

2 batches pizza dough (page 179 or store bought)

2 cups mozzarella cheese

1 cup shredded Cheddar cheese

½ cup chopped cilantro

CHICKEN

1. In a large frying pan on medium-high heat, cook the chicken and diced onions in the oil for about for 15 minutes, until the chicken and onions start to brown.

2. Add the vinegar and barbecue sauce. Stir to combine and scrape the bottom of the pan to incorporate any browned bits stuck to the pan.

3. Cover and simmer for 30 minutes, stirring occasionally, until the chicken becomes tender and falls apart.

4. Remove the chicken and shred it. Return the shredded meat to the pot and stir. Set aside.

CONTINUED ➡

5.   Preheat the oven to 350°F.

6.   Divide the dough in half and roll one half out about ¼-inch thick.

7.   Cut rounds of dough the same size as the pan you will use to cook the pizza. It's easiest to use the pan itself as a cookie cutter. Cut 5 rounds.

8.   Allow the dough to shrink a little after you cut it. This might happen naturally, depending on the elasticity and temperature of the dough, but if it doesn't, cut about half an inch off the radius of the circle.

9.   Line a baking sheet with parchment and lightly grease the paper.

10. Place the 5 rounds of dough onto the baking sheet, side by side. Bake for 15 minutes, until cooked and slightly brown.

11. Meanwhile, line the pan you are using for the cake with parchment and lightly grease the paper.

12. Incorporate the leftover dough scraps from the first half of the dough into the second half.

13. Roll it out to about ½-inch thickness.

14. Cut a round a little bit bigger than the pizza cake can from one of the edges of the dough. Press the round into the bottom of the pizza cake pan.

15. Cut 3 strips of dough to have the same width as the height of the baking dish, which should be about 8 inches.

16. Drape the strips of dough sideways, one by one, around the rim of the pan. As you go, secure the bottom of the dough strips to the bottom dough round. As you add each strip, seal them together so you have one uniform piece of dough.

17. Pour about one-sixth of the barbecue chicken mixture into the pizza cake dough shell, then about one-sixth each of the cheese, sliced onion, and cilantro.

18. Top with the first baked round of dough. Top with more chicken mix, cheese, onion, and cilantro and repeat until you use all of the baked dough rounds and fillings.

19. Cut off the excess hanging dough.

20. Bake for 45 minutes.

21. Allow to rest for 15 minutes before slicing and serving.

THE INGREDIENTS OF
BARBECUE CHICKEN
COMBINED WITH

THE INGREDIENTS
OF PIZZA CAKE
MAKE

New
Mash-up!

BARBECUE CHICKEN

PIZZA CAKE

SIDES

ISAAN STEAK PASTA SALAD

MAKES	PREP TIME	COOK TIME	TOTAL TIME
8 to 10 servings	30 minutes	20 minutes	50 minutes

The first time I had Isaan steak salad was a revelation. *Oh, this is how Thai food is supposed to taste! I get it now!* This insanely bright and fresh dish is bursting with flavor. I wanted to eat it as a meal, but it's just a pile of beef, so I added pasta. If you do eat it as a meal, the recipe below makes about 3 or 4 servings.

1. Mix the fish sauce, soy sauce, vinegar, lime juice, Sriracha, honey, and lemongrass and marinate the steak in the mixture for at least 30 minutes and up to 3 hours.

2. On a grill or in a cast iron pan, cook the steak on high heat for about 5 minutes per side to medium doneness.

3. Allow the steak to rest for about 10 minutes before slicing it very thin against the grain. Collect the juices.

4. In a large bowl, mix the steak juices, fish sauce, lime juice, and the sliced steak.

5. Boil a pot of water and cook the pasta al dente.

6. Strain and immediately toss the pasta with the steak and juices. Add the Fresno chiles.

7. Allow to cool fully in the fridge, about 1 hour.

8. Stir in the mint and cilantro.

STEAK

2 tablespoons fish sauce

2 tablespoons soy sauce

1 tablespoon rice vinegar

juice of 2 limes

1 tablespoon Sriracha

2 tablespoons honey

4 stalks lemongrass, thick outer husks removed, chopped

1 pound skirt steak

SALAD

¼ cup fish sauce

¼ cup lime juice

1 pound penne

5 Fresno chiles, sliced into thin rounds

½ cup chopped mint

½ cup chopped cilantro

VIETNAMESE TABBOULEH

MAKES	PREP TIME	COOK TIME	TOTAL TIME
8 to 10 servings	30 minutes	10 minutes	40 minutes

This couscous salad uses bun vermicelli for its flavor profile. The super fresh flavors complement any backyard barbecue, and it's also great in a big batch for lunch throughout the week.

1. Boil a pot of water and cook the couscous for about 10 minutes, until tender. Strain.

2. Add the remaining ingredients to the couscous and toss to combine.

3. Refrigerate for at least 30 minutes before serving.

1 pound Israeli couscous

1 cup chopped peanuts

½ cup chopped mint

½ cup chopped basil

1 cup chopped romaine hearts

1 cucumber, diced

2 carrots, diced

¼ cup Sriracha

¼ cup fish sauce

2 tablespoons honey

¼ cup lime juice

THE INGREDIENTS OF BUN VERMICELLI COMBINED WITH ➡

THE INGREDIENTS OF TABBOULEH MAKE ➡

New Mash-up!

VIETNAMESE TABBOULEH

LOADED POTATO MOFONGO

MAKES	PREP TIME	COOK TIME	TOTAL TIME
4 servings	20 minutes	15 minutes	35 minutes

Springfield, Massachusetts, has a vibrant Puerto Rican culture, which introduced me to mofongo at an early age. This lump of dry mashed plantain is a vehicle to get garlic and pork rinds into your face. I made it with bacon instead of pork rinds one day, and it made me think of mashed potatoes, so I served it with sour cream, chives, and more bacon. The stock and sour cream in the plantain mixture keep it from tasting too dry.

canola or peanut oil for frying

3 yellow-green plantains, peeled and chopped into 1-inch rounds

8 ounces bacon

2 cloves garlic

salt and pepper

½ cup chicken stock

1 tablespoon apple cider vinegar

½ cup sour cream, plus more for serving

¼ cup chopped chives

1. In a frying pan, pour oil about ½-inch deep and heat it to 350°F.

2. Add the plantains to the oil and fry about 5 minutes, flipping once, until lightly brown and tender in the center. Remove from the oil and dry on a paper towel.

3. Meanwhile, in another frying pan, cook the bacon on medium-high heat for about 5 minutes, flipping occasionally, until crispy. Remove from the pan and dry on a paper towel. Reserve 2 tablespoons of the bacon fat. Discard or store the excess for another use.

4. With a mortar and pestle, mash the garlic and reserved bacon fat into a paste.

5. Add the fried plantains to the bacon frying pan and season with salt and pepper. Mash until smooth.

6. Add half the bacon and continue mashing.

7. In small increments, add the stock, vinegar, and sour cream and continue mashing. Make sure the additions incorporate before adding more. Taste as you go and stop when it becomes softer than peanut butter and has a strong, salty, creamy flavor.

8. Top with the rest of the bacon, sour cream, and chives.

FAST-FOOD BURGER STUFFING

MAKES	PREP TIME	COOK TIME	TOTAL TIME
10 servings	30 minutes	1 hour	1 hour 30 minutes

Big Mac® burgers are delicious. We can be food snobs and pretend that they aren't, but food scientists developed the Big Mac to achieve optimal deliciousness. If you don't believe me, you probably haven't had one in a while and you probably haven't had one while drunk in a while. This recipe came to me a few weeks after Thanksgiving one year when I was eating a Big Mac (and probably drunk). What makes the burger good? It's not the burger itself—of course not. It has to do with the interplay of cheap bread, cheese, pickles, and crunchy lettuce. The ratios of meat, bread, and flavorings approximate stuffing, so why not buy eight Big Macs, chop them up, stir in some chicken stock, and bake it to make stuffing? After I sobered up, I didn't want to spend $40 at McDonald's, but I did have almost a whole year to think about the recipe. There's no question that you're eating stuffing and no question that it tastes like a Big Mac. It's absolutely amazing.

1. Preheat the oven to 325°F.

2. Chop the buns into small cubes, lay them on large baking sheet, and bake for about 30 minutes, stirring occasionally, to dehydrate them and brown them lightly.

3. Meanwhile, combine all of the sauce ingredients and whisk or beat vigorously with a fork.

4. In a frying pan, melt the butter and add the beef with ample salt and pepper. Fully brown and cook the beef [heat level how long] and remove from the heat.

5. In a large bowl, mix the bread with the beef-butter mixture. Add the onion, pickles, and then the sauce. Stir well and pour into a baking dish.

6. Bake for 30 minutes.

7. Top with lettuce and serve hot.

8 sesame seed buns (the cheap kind)

SAUCE

5 large dill pickle chips, finely diced

1 teaspoon grated white onion

1 teaspoon paprika

½ teaspoon grated garlic

½ cup chicken stock

½ cup mayonnaise

1 egg, beaten

1 tablespoon ketchup

1 tablespoon pickle juice

1 tablespoon Sriracha

½ tablespoon mustard

STUFFING

4 tablespoons butter

12 ounces lean ground beef

salt and pepper

4 ounces Cheddar cheese

½ cup diced white onion

½ cup diced pickles

½ head iceberg lettuce, finely shredded

CORN CHOWDER POLENTA

MAKES	PREP TIME	COOK TIME	TOTAL TIME
6 servings	10 minutes	35 minutes	45 minutes

Using a soup as the liquid for polenta or risotto is an easy way to mash up recipes. Polenta comes from corn, which makes it a great vehicle for a corn chowder. This recipe is a bowl of pure comfort after a long, cold day.

½ pound bacon, chopped

1 large yellow onion, diced

1 large carrot, diced

2 stalks celery, diced

2 Yukon Gold potatoes, diced

1 red bell pepper, diced

2 tablespoons butter

2 cloves garlic, minced

1 cup cream

1 quart chicken stock

1 quart whole milk

2 cups corn kernels

2¼ cups cornmeal

½ cup grated Parmesan cheese

¼ cup chopped parsley

salt and pepper

red pepper flakes

1. In a heavy-bottomed pan on medium-high heat, cook the bacon for about 5 minutes, until the fat renders and the bacon becomes crispy. Remove from the pan.

2. Retain 1 tablespoon of the bacon fat to cook the veggies. Discard or store the excess for another use.

3. Sauté the onion, carrot, celery, potatoes, and bell pepper in the butter and the reserved bacon fat on medium-high heat for about 10 minutes.

4. Add the garlic and cook for 1 minute.

5. Add the cream, stock, and milk. Bring to a simmer and add the corn kernels and cornmeal. Stir vigorously to remove any lumps. You want a smooth mixture.

6. Reduce the heat to low and stir until the cornmeal becomes tender, about 25 minutes, depending on the coarseness of your cornmeal.

7. Return the bacon to the mixture and stir in the Parmesan cheese and parsley.

8. Add salt, pepper, and red pepper flakes to taste.

 THE INGREDIENTS OF CORN CHOWDER COMBINED WITH ➡

 THE INGREDIENTS OF POLENTA MAKE ➡

 New Mash-up! CORN CHOWDER POLENTA

Mix It Up!

Polenta, grits, and risotto have great mash-up potential. They all use a similar process, cook with a flavorful liquid, and mix in ingredients. Here's a selection of similar dishes and how you might approach them.

Buffalo Chicken ➡ cooking liquid: broth, butter, and cayenne hot sauce
mix in: shredded chicken, carrot, celery, blue cheese

Cheeseburger ➡ cooking liquid: beef broth
mix in: ground beef, tomato, onion, pickles, cheese

Corned Beef & Cabbage ➡ cooking liquid: corned beef broth
mix in: corned beef, cabbage, carrots

Fried Rice ➡ cooking liquid: broth with soy sauce, rice vinegar, and sesame oil
mix in: pork, peas, onion, chile peppers, scallions

Green Curry ➡ cooking liquid: coconut milk and green curry paste
mix in: protein of choice, veggies, basil

Pizza ➡ cooking liquid: tomato sauce and stock
mix in: sausage, peppers, pepperoni, cheese

Thanksgiving ➡ cooking liquid: turkey stock
mix in: turkey, cranberries, green beans, squash

BREAKFAST

CARBONARA EGGS BENEDICT

MAKES	PREP TIME	COOK TIME	TOTAL TIME
4 benedicts	1 hour 30 minutes	15 minutes	1 hour 45 minutes

Carbonara is basically bacon and eggs pasta, so I love mashing it up with breakfast dishes. One of my favorite dishes with one of my favorite meals—so you can imagine my excitement about this recipe. The crispy, eggy pasta goes so well with the creamy hollandaise sauce and runny egg yolk, creating carbonara magic with every bite.

SPAGHETTI ROUNDS

1. Cook the bacon on medium-high heat for about 5 minutes, flipping occasionally, until crispy. Remove bacon slices from the pan and save them for building the benedict. Reserve 2 tablespoons bacon fat and retain the rest in the pan for browning the pasta rounds (step 11).

2. In a large bowl, mix the 2 tablespoons of fat with the egg yolks, egg, Pecorino Romano, and black pepper and mix well.

3. Boil a pot of water and cook the pasta.

4. Transfer the noodles from the pot into the egg mixture. Stir well to combine and allow the eggs to cook lightly from the residual heat.

5. Grease four round plastic storage containers with the same circumference as an English muffin. Takeout containers work great.

6. Use a large fork to spool a quarter of the pasta, as if you were swirling the biggest bite ever. Allow the pasta to drop off the fork and fill each container in a spiral shape. Refrigerate the pasta rounds for at least 1 hour or preferably overnight.

HOLLANDAISE SAUCE

7. Whisk the yolks with the lemon juice until the mixture lightens in color and fluffs up a bit.

8. Place the lemon-yolk mixture in a double boiler and slowly whisk in the melted butter.

SPAGHETTI ROUNDS

8 slices bacon

2 egg yolks

1 egg

½ cup grated Pecorino Romano cheese

2 tablespoons freshly cracked black pepper

½ pound spaghetti

HOLLANDAISE SAUCE

4 egg yolks

juice of 1 lemon

8 tablespoons butter, melted

THE REST

2 English muffins

4 eggs

¼ cup grated Parmesan cheese

pepper

CONTINUED →

9. Continue whisking until the mixture thickens and reaches an internal temperature of around 135°F. Add more lemon juice or a splash of water if it thickens too much.

10. Turn off the heat beneath the double boiler but keep the sauce in the warm double boiler until ready to use.

THE REST

11. In the frying pan with the retained bacon fat, brown both sides of the chilled pasta rounds on medium-high heat, about 3–5 minutes per side.

12. Split the English muffins into halves and toast them.

13. Bring a small pot of water to a simmer.

14. Crack each egg into a mesh strainer and shake off excess egg white that slides through the strainer.

15. Gently dip the strainer into the simmering water. Poach for about 3 minutes, occasionally shaking the egg off the strainer.

16. Remove the eggs from the water with a slotted spoon.

17. Build the benedict by layering a muffin half, the bacon, pasta, Parmesan cheese, poached egg, and hollandaise sauce.

18. Top with freshly ground black pepper.

THE INGREDIENTS
OF CARBONARA
COMBINED WITH

THE INGREDIENTS
OF EGGS BENEDICT
MAKE

New
Mash-up!

CARBONARA

EGGS BENEDICT

PASTA FAGIOLI FRITTATA

MAKES	PREP TIME	COOK TIME	TOTAL TIME
1 frittata, 8 to 10 servings	30 minutes	30 minutes	1 hour

This recipe started my obsession with eating pasta for breakfast. The first time I put pasta into a frittata it was so good and I was so excited with how it tasted that I started putting it in all my breakfasts. This version tastes like the pasta fagioli my grandmother used to make when I was growing up.

1. Boil a pot of water and cook the ditalini al dente.

2. In a large bowl, beat the eggs.

3. Add the pasta, mozzarella, Parmesean, beans, and parsley and mix well.

4. Preheat the oven to 350°F.

5. In a large oven-safe frying pan, cook the sausage, onion, celery, and carrot over medium-high heat for about 10 minutes to brown and cook through.

6. Add garlic and cook 2 minutes.

7. Stir in the tomatoes and scrape any residue from the bottom of the pan. Cook another 5 minutes.

8. Transfer the meat and veggies from the pan into the bowl with the egg mixture and stir to combine.

9. Wipe the pan dry, add a little oil, and heat the oil on high until it ripples in the pan.

10. Add the pasta mixture to the pan and transfer it immediately into the oven.

11. Bake it for 30 minutes, until it sets but doesn't dry out.

12. Allow to sit for 10 minutes before cutting and serving.

¾ pound ditalini

8 eggs

1 cup shredded mozzarella cheese

½ cup grated Parmesan cheese

1 (15-ounce) can pink beans, drained and rinsed

¼ cup chopped parsley

½ pound hot Italian sausage

1 small yellow onion, diced

2 stalks celery, diced

1 carrot, diced

2 cloves garlic, minced

1 (28-ounce) can diced tomatoes, strained

olive oil

BREAKFAST POUTINE

MAKES	PREP TIME	COOK TIME	TOTAL TIME
2 servings	30 minutes	15 minutes	45 minutes

Every kid dreams of French fries for breakfast. They're also an instant hangover cure. Poutine consists of fries, gravy, and cheese. For the gravy element, this recipe uses sausage gravy. Cheddar cheese goes into the mix perfectly, but, in true poutine tradition, keep it unmelted. These aren't cheese fries, people! The egg on top makes it perfect.

1. Peel the potatoes and slice them into ½-inch French fries.

2. Place the fries in a bowl of water, stir them around, and strain.

3. Repeat step 2 but allow them to soak for 15 minutes before straining. Dry thoroughly with paper towels.

4. Meanwhile, in a frying pan, melt 1 tablespoon of the butter, add the onion, salt, and pepper, and cook for about 10 minutes on medium-high heat to brown the onion lightly around the edges.

5. Add the sausage and cook another 5 minutes.

6. Add the flour and stir well to combine. Cook for about 3 minutes to cook the raw flavor out of the flour.

7. Whisk in the milk and bring to a simmer to thicken. If the mixture thickens too much, add a splash of milk to thin it out. Season with salt and pepper as needed.

8. Stir in the parsley and remove from the heat.

9. Preheat the oil to 350°F.

10. Strain the fries and dry them thoroughly with paper towels.

11. Add the fries to the oil and fry for about 8 minutes, until tender. Remove from the oil and place on a drying rack.

12. Increase the frying oil temperature to 425°F. Fry the fries for 5 minutes to brown and crisp them.

13. Remove the fries from the oil to the drying rack and season with salt and pepper.

14. In a nonstick pan, melt the remaining 1 tablespoon of butter and fry the egg, sunny side up.

15. Place the fries in a bowl or on a serving dish. Top with the gravy, cheese, and then the fried egg.

2 large russet potatoes

2 tablespoons butter, divided

1 small yellow onion, diced

salt and pepper

¼ pound breakfast sausage

1 tablespoon all-purpose flour

1 cup whole milk, plus more as needed

¼ cup chopped parsley

canola or peanut oil for frying

1 egg

½ cup grated Cheddar cheese

BREAKFAST RAMEN

MAKES	PREP TIME	COOK TIME	TOTAL TIME
2 bowls	30 minutes	15 minutes	45 minutes

What I call "cheater's ramen" consists of store-bought chicken stock modified with soy sauce, vinegar, and Sriracha. It can satisfy a ramen craving without having to go to a restaurant or resorting to the instant stuff. It also works in this recipe because there's no reason to boil pork bones for 18 hours just for a fun riff on breakfast.

NOODLE LOGIC➡ If you don't have an Asian market in your area or you can't find fresh ramen noodles at your grocery store, buy 2 packets of instant ramen noodle soup, use the noodles, and discard the flavor packets or save them for another use.

1 quart chicken stock

2 tablespoons soy sauce

1 tablespoon rice vinegar

1 tablespoon Sriracha

2 teaspoons sesame oil

1 large russet potato

4 slices bacon

6 ounces ramen noodles

2 eggs

scallion for garnish

1. Boil a pot of water for the noodles.

2. Meanwhile, bring the stock to a simmer and stir in the soy sauce, vinegar, Sriracha, and sesame oil.

3. Stab fork holes into the potato and microwave it on high for 5 minutes.

4. Cut potato into ½-inch cubes.

5. In a frying pan on medium-high heat, cook the bacon for 5 minutes, until crispy. Remove from the pan and dry on a paper towel. Retain the bacon fat in the pan.

6. Add the potatoes to the pan with the bacon fat. Cook on high for about 10 minutes, stirring and flipping often, to brown them well. Remove from the heat.

7. Meanwhile, drop the noodles into the boiling water. Cook for 3 to 5 minutes, depending on the brand or type of noodles, then strain.

8. Fry the eggs, sunny side up.

9. Build the bowls with the noodles, stock, potatoes, bacon, and egg.

10. Top with chopped scallion.

CRISPY RICE STICKY BUNS

MAKES	PREP TIME	COOK TIME	TOTAL TIME
8 large buns	9 hours	45 minutes	9 hours and 45 minutes

"Gooey" and "sticky" apply equally to crispy rice treats and sticky buns, so I thought it would be fun to see what a mash-up of these dishes would look like. The cereal sort of takes the place of pecans, and marshmallows function as the sticky part. The buns come out sticky, chewy, and crunchy all at the same time—exactly how a Crispy Rice Sticky Bun should taste.

SHE BEAT BOBBY FLAY WITH THIS ONE→ I adapted the brioche dough and overall method for this recipe from Joanne Chang of Flour Bakery + Café in Boston.

DOUGH

1. Using a stand mixer with a dough hook, combine the flour, yeast, sugar, salt, and eggs with ½ cup of cold water. Beat on low for about 8 minutes, stopping to scrape the sides and help the dough come together as often as needed. The dough will look dry.

2. Still on low speed, add the butter cubes one piece at a time. Wait until each cube completely incorporates before adding the next.

3. Once all the butter combines, increase the mixer speed to medium and beat for about 15 minutes, until the dough goes from looking flaky and weird to nice and smooth.

4. Put the dough in a greased container and cover. Allow to rest at least 8 hours or overnight in the fridge.

CRISPY RICE

5. Pour the cereal into a large mixing bowl.

6. In a medium pot, melt the butter and marshmallows on low heat for about 5 minutes, until it becomes a uniform texture.

7. Pour the marshmallow mixture into the cereal bowl and stir vigorously to combine.

8. On a piece of wax paper, press the crispy rice mixture into a thin 12 × 16-inch rectangle.

BRIOCHE DOUGH

4 ½ cups all-purpose flour, plus extra for rolling

1 ½ packets active dry yeast (3 ¼ teaspoons)

⅓ cup sugar

1 tablespoon salt

6 eggs

½ pound butter, plus 4 tablespoons, room temperature and cut into cubes

1 teaspoon cinnamon

CRISPY RICE

6 cups puffed rice cereal

4 tablespoons butter

10 ounces marshmallows

SAUCE

10 ounces marshmallows

4 tablespoons butter, melted

½ cup honey

SAUCE

9. In a large bowl, mix the marshmallows, melted butter, and honey and toss to coat the marshmallows. Pour the coated marshmallows into a 9 × 13-inch baking dish.

ROLLS

10. On a lightly floured surface, roll the brioche dough out into a 12 × 16-inch rectangle.

11. Sprinkle the cinnamon onto the dough.

12. Transfer the crispy rice mixture onto the dough.

13. Roll the dough widthwise into a tight spiral. Don't worry if some of the crispy rice pieces stick through the dough.

14. Cut the log into 8 (2-inch) sticky buns and place each bun into the baking dish containing the uncooked marshmallow sauce. Tuck the buns in a little.

15. Allow the buns to rise at room temperature for 30 minutes.

16. Preheat the oven to 350°F.

17. Bake the buns for 35 to 45 minutes, until golden.

18. Allow to cool for 30 minutes.

19. To serve, invert the buns onto a plate and scoop some of the extra sauce on top of the buns.

THE INGREDIENTS OF CRISPY RICE TREATS
COMBINED WITH

↓

THE INGREDIENTS OF STICKY BUNS
MAKE

↓

New Mash-up!

CRISPY RICE STICKY BUNS

SWEETS

THAI MASSAMAN COOKIES

MAKES	PREP TIME	COOK TIME	TOTAL TIME
24 cookies	1 hour 30 minutes	12 minutes	1 hour 42 minutes

The ingredients of massaman curry sound more like a dessert than a main dish, right? To make this mash-up, I used a simple peanut butter cookie recipe and added the spices and coconut . . . plus some chiles to remind you that this recipe comes from a curry. Korean-style chile flakes are fun because the large specks of bright red are still visible in the finished cookie, but feel free to use the chile flakes of your choice.

HACKING COCONUT CREAM➡ You can buy coconut cream in the grocery store, but it can prove hard to find in some areas. If that's the case, you can hack it—literally. Put a can of coconut milk in the fridge overnight. The next day, the cream will have risen to the top and hardened.

4 tablespoons butter, room temperature

¼ cup coconut cream

½ cup sugar

½ cup packed brown sugar

½ cup peanut butter

1 egg

1¼ cups all-purpose flour

¾ teaspoon baking soda

½ teaspoon baking powder

1 pinch salt

2 tablespoons minced candied ginger

1 teaspoon cardamom

½ teaspoon cinnamon

¼ cup shredded sweetened coconut flakes

½ teaspoon Korean-style chile flakes

1 tablespoon grated lime zest, plus more for garnish

1. In a bowl or with a stand mixer, fully combine the butter, coconut cream, and sugars.

2. Stir in the peanut butter.

3. Whisk the egg and then stir it in.

4. Mix the flour, baking soda, and baking powder together and then stir into the mixture.

5. Add the salt, ginger, cardamom, cinnamon, coconut flakes, chile flakes, and lime zest. Refrigerate for 1 hour.

6. Preheat the oven to 350°F.

7. Shape the chilled dough into 1½-inch balls and place on a lined and greased cookie sheet.

8. Bake for about 12 minutes, until the cookies just start to brown around the edges.

9. Remove from the oven and let cool.

10. Garnish with additional lime zest.

BOSTON CREAM FRIED DOUGH

MAKES	PREP TIME	COOK TIME	TOTAL TIME
4 fried doughs	4 hours 20 minutes	10 minutes	4 hours 30 minutes

A little cart in the center of Boston has sold Boston cream fried dough for a long time. That mash-up pioneer was doing it long before most people. Plus, if you think about it, Boston cream donuts already mash-up donuts and Boston cream pie.

PASTRY CREAM

1. Beat the yolks and egg with the sugar and cornstarch until light and fluffy.

2. Heat the milk to a simmer and remove from the heat.

3. Stream the milk into the egg mixture while whisking.

4. Bring the custard mixture to a simmer, whisking constantly. It will thicken.

5. Remove from the heat and add the vanilla, butter, and salt.

6. Strain through a mesh strainer to remove any clumps.

7. Cover with plastic wrap touching the surface of the mixture to avoid a skin forming and chill for 4 hours.

GANACHE

8. In a bowl, mix the chocolate, cream, and butter and microwave on high for 20 seconds.

9. Stir and repeat until smooth, but do not microwave too long. Stir thoroughly after each heating. The chocolate will melt pretty quickly, and you can stir out the smaller lumps. If you overheat it, it will be unusable. If the chocolate seems too thin or thick, add more chocolate or cream to balance it out.

DOUGH

10. Pour 1 inch of oil into a frying pan and heat it to 350°F.

PASTRY CREAM

2 egg yolks

1 egg

½ cup sugar

¼ cup cornstarch

2¼ cups milk

2 teaspoons vanilla extract

2 tablespoons butter

1 pinch salt

GANACHE

6 ounces dark chocolate

1 cup heavy cream

1 tablespoon butter

SAUCE

10 ounces marshmallows

4 tablespoons butter, melted

½ cup honey

OTHER

canola or peanut oil for frying

pizza dough (page 179 or store bought)

11. Divide the dough into fourths and form each into a round about 8 to 10 inches in diameter.

12. Fry each round on both sides for about 2 minutes per side, until brown and cooked through.

13. Divide the chocolate onto the dough rounds.

14. With a piping bag or clean plastic storage bag with one corner snipped off, add the pastry cream in wide lines.

15. Use a toothpick to make dents in the cream, moving perpendicular to the lines to form a marbleized design.

WHITE RUSSIAN CHEESECAKE

MAKES	PREP TIME	COOK TIME	TOTAL TIME
1 cheesecake, 8 servings	5 hours 30 minutes	1 hour	6 hours 30 minutes

The White Russian cocktail goes in and out of style. I always forget how much I love it until I drink a perfectly made one. It tastes milky with just a hint of coffee and booze, which perfectly matches a cheesecake. With most foods or desserts that contain booze, you can't really taste the alcohol, but in this cake you can—and that's a good thing.

CAKE

1. Preheat the oven to 350°F.

2. In a food processor, pulse the cookies until crumbled. Add butter and pulse into a batter.

3. In a tart pan or springform pan, spread the cookie batter on the bottom and sides to form the crust.

4. Bake for 10 minutes. Remove from the oven and allow to cool.

5. In a food processor, pulse the cream cheese, sour cream, milk, and sugar until smooth. While the machine is on, slowly add the liqueur and vodka and then the eggs, one at a time.

6. Pour the filling into the cookie crust and bake about 1 hour, until just set.

7. Chill the cake for at least 5 hours and up to 2 days.

CARAMEL

8. In a small pot, pour ½ cup water, add sugar, and put over high heat. Occasionally swirl the pan around but don't stir. Cook about 15 minutes until the mixture browns but hasn't burned. No stirring!

9. Add the cream and whisk while the mixture bubbles. It will bubble up the sides of the pot and possibly splatter. This mixture is HOT.

10. Once the caramel is smooth, add the salt and whisk to combine.

11. Pour the warm caramel over the chilled cake.

CHEESECAKE

⅔ package chocolate sandwich cookies

½ stick butter, room temperature

16 ounces cream cheese

⅔ cup sour cream

1 cup sugar

⅔ cup milk

1 cup coffee liqueur

2 tablespoons vodka

4 eggs

CARAMEL

1 cup sugar

½ cup cream

1 teaspoon salt

CAPRESE SUNDAE

MAKES	PREP TIME	COOK TIME	TOTAL TIME
3 sundaes	2 hours 20 minutes	2 hours	4 hours 20 minutes

I tried a tomato jam that I had made on vanilla ice cream, and it tasted great. Basil also tastes great in desserts, which got me thinking. I was two-thirds of the way to a full caprese. Might as well squeeze in the mozzarella somewhere—like ice cream. This ice cream has a really interesting texture: It seems like the cheese melts right into the mixture, but when you take a bite it still has tiny pieces of cheese in there that you can chew and squeak like eating fresh mozzarella.

JAM

1. Bring a pot of water to a boil.

2. Core the top of the tomatoes and score the bottoms with an X.

3. Boil the tomatoes for about 2 minutes, until the skin starts to peel away.

4. Remove the tomatoes from the pot and discard the water.

5. Peel the tomatoes and add them back into the pot along with the sugar, honey, and salt.

6. Cook on low for about 2 hours, until the mixture forms a nice jammy consistency.

7. Add the lemon juice and chill until ready to use.

ICE CREAM

8. In a pot on the stove or in the microwave in a heat-proof bowl, heat the milk and cream on low until the liquid is steaming and just about to simmer.

9. Meanwhile, break up the cheese with your fingers to almost a paste. Nice fresh mozzarella in water should break down easily.

10. In a small bowl, mix the sugar, milk powder, and xanthan gum.

TOMATO JAM

5 large vine-ripened tomatoes

½ cup sugar

¼ cup honey

1 pinch salt

juice of 1 lemon

MOZZARELLA ICE CREAM

1 cup milk

1 cup cream

4 ounces fresh mozzarella

½ cup sugar

½ cup nonfat milk powder

1/8 teaspoon xanthan gum

BASIL WHIPPED CREAM

1 cup heavy whipping cream

2 basil branches

15 leaves basil, plus 3 more for garnish

2 tablespoons sugar

CONTINUED ➡

11. When the milk just barely starts to simmer, remove from the heat and whisk in the sugar mixture followed by the mozzarella. Continue whisking until everything combines and dissolves.

12. Refrigerate the mozzarella mixture for 1 hour, then transfer it to the freezer for 30 minutes, until just below freezing.

13. Pour into an ice cream maker and freeze according to the manufacturer's instructions.

14. Return to the freezer until it becomes scoopable, about 2 hours.

WHIPPED CREAM

15. In a pot on the stove or in the microwave in a heat-proof bowl, heat the cream until it's steaming and just about to simmer.

16. Add the basil branches to steep. Refrigerate 8 hours or overnight.

17. Mince the basil leaves as small as you can.

18. Remove the basil branches from the cream.

19. Add the basil leaves and sugar to the cream.

20. Whisk or beat the basil cream until peaks form and you have scoopable whipped cream.

SUNDAE

21. In a heat-proof bowl, heat the tomato jam in the microwave on high for about 1 minute.

22. Scoop some ice cream into a bowl and pour the tomato jam over the top.

23. Top with the whipped cream and a basil leaf for garnish.

THE INGREDIENTS OF CAPRESE SALAD COMBINED WITH

THE INGREDIENTS OF AN ICE CREAM SUNDAE MAKE

New Mash-up!

CAPRESE SUNDAE

CEREAL BOWL PANNA COTTA

MAKES	PREP TIME	COOK TIME	TOTAL TIME
5 servings	4 hours 15 minutes	10 minutes	4 hours 25 minutes

I love ice cream. When the Cereal Milk Ice Cream at Momofuku Milk Bar changed the game, I started thinking of new ways to use the concept. For this recipe, I like using the super sugary cereals that my parents never let me eat when I was a kid to make it an extra-special treat.

1. In a medium bowl, pour 1 cup of the cream and 1 cup of the milk over the chocolate cereal.

2. In another medium bowl, pour the remaining 1 cup of cream and the remaining 1 cup of milk over the peanut butter cereal. Allow both to sit for 1 hour.

3. In a small bowl, mix half the gelatin and 1½ tablespoons of water. Repeat with the other half in another bowl.

4. Strain out the chocolate cereal and either discard or store for another use.

5. Transfer the chocolate cereal milk into a saucepan and bring to a simmer, whisking often. Add the cocoa powder and simmer for 5 minutes. Remove from the heat and whisk in half of the gelatin.

6. Divide the chocolate liquid evenly into 5 buttered ramekins. Fill them only about halfway. Allow to cool for 30 minutes in the freezer.

7. Repeat steps 4 and 5 with the peanut butter cereal and milk, omitting the cocoa powder.

8. Slowly pour the peanut butter milk mixture over the top of the chocolate portion, filling the ramekins the rest of the way.

9. Refrigerate the ramekins for 2½ half hours.

10. To serve, invert onto a plate and garnish with crumbled cereal.

2 cups cream, divided

2 cups milk, divided

1½ cups chocolate cereal, plus more for garnish

1½ cups peanut butter cereal, plus more for garnish

2½ teaspoons (1 packet) unflavored gelatin, divided

1 tablespoon cocoa powder

butter for greasing

ICE CREAM TACOS

MAKES	PREP TIME	COOK TIME	TOTAL TIME
about 10 tacos	3 hours 30 minutes	30 minutes	4 hours

Any self-respecting ice cream truck serves choco tacos, a handheld twist on an ice cream cone. My favorite version of this clever mash-up adds cookies and cream and coconut flavors into the mix. If you don't have a pizzelle maker, use a hot nonstick pan as if making crepes. Add a few tablespoons of milk until the shell batter resembles pancake batter and pour it into the pan. After about 1 minute, flip it and cook another minute. Remove from the pan and form the taco shape until it hardens.

TOASTED VS. BURNED ➡ I sometimes burn my coconut when toasting it because I like it nice and brown, and the line between dark toasted and burnt is thin. Once it starts browning, keep a close eye on it because it can burn really easily.

ICE CREAM

1. In a pot on the stove or in the microwave in a heat-proof bowl, heat the milk and cream on low until the liquid is steaming and just about to simmer.

2. In a small bowl, mix the sugar, milk powder, and xanthan gum.

3. When the milk just barely starts to simmer, remove from the heat and whisk in the sugar mixture followed by the coconut paste. Continue whisking until the new mixture combines and everything dissolves. Be careful with the coconut paste because different brands can have different strengths. Taste as you go and use as little or as much as you need for the desired flavor.

4. Refrigerate the coconut mixture for 1 hour, then transfer it to the freezer for 30 minutes, until just below freezing.

5. Pour into an ice cream maker and freeze according to the manufacturer's instructions

6. Stir in the cookies.

7. Return to the freezer until it becomes spreadable, about 1 hour.

ICE CREAM

2 cups milk

2 cups cream

1¼ cups sugar

1 cup nonfat milk powder

⅛ teaspoon xanthan gum

1 pinch salt

1 teaspoon coconut extract paste

1 cup crushed chocolate sandwich cookies

SHELLS

2 egg whites

½ cup sugar

½ teaspoon vanilla extract

1 pinch salt

½ cup all-purpose flour

2 tablespoons melted unsalted butter

3 tablespoons cocoa powder

3 cups sweetened coconut flakes

1 tablespoon coconut oil

CONTINUED ➡

8. Preheat the pizzelle maker.

9. Whisk the egg whites in a bowl until smooth.

10. Whisk the sugar, vanilla, salt, and flour into the egg whites until they incorporate.

11. Stir in the butter and then the cocoa powder.

12. Pour 1 tablespoon of shell batter into the pizzelle maker, close it, and cook for about 1 ½ minutes.

13. Open and form a taco shape with a book or thick wooden spoon. It should harden after about 30 seconds. If the taco seems too brittle, cook the next one for less time. If it seems too soft, cook it a little more. Once you get the hang of it, you can make more at a time if your machine can handle it.

TACOS

14. Scoop some ice cream into the taco shell. Place the stuffed shell onto a tray or in a small plastic storage bag and put it in the freezer.

15. Preheat the oven to 350°F.

16. Coat the coconut flakes with the oil and spread evenly on a baking sheet.

17. Bake for about 5 minutes and take them out to stir.

18. Continue to bake, checking and stirring every few minutes, until they toast evenly.

19. When ready to serve, remove the tacos from the freezer and top with the toasted coconut flakes.

THE INGREDIENTS OF COOKIES AND CREAM ICE CREAM
COMBINED WITH

THE INGREDIENTS OF TACOS
MAKE

New Smash-in!

ICE CREAM TACOS

PB&J ICE CREAM SANDWICH

MAKES	PREP TIME	COOK TIME	TOTAL TIME
24 sandwiches	10 hours 45 minutes	15 minutes	11 hours

Once you start making ice cream, it's a hard habit to kick. I came up with this peanut butter and jelly ice cream sandwich at the gelato company where I worked as a production manager for two years. We sold them on a few occasions, which made me proud. The flavors are absolutely classic and will remind you of childhood, as any good dessert should.

GOOD MILK MAKES GOOD ICE CREAM ➡ Buy good milk. Invest in a local, organic brand so you can taste the milk flavor in your ice cream. It makes a huge difference.

COOKIE

1. In the bowl of a stand mixer, sift the flour and baking soda together.

2. Add the butter, brown sugar, and granulated sugar and beat on medium-high speed until pale and fluffy, about 4 minutes.

3. Beat in the eggs one at a time, then add the vanilla and salt.

4. Wrap with plastic and refrigerate for 1 hour.

5. Preheat the oven to 350°F.

6. Grease a half sheet pan and line with greased parchment.

7. Spread the cookie mixture evenly over the whole pan. Bake for about 15 minutes, until it sets.

8. Freeze for at least 15 minutes before you build the sandwiches.

ICE CREAM

9. Combine the milk and cream in a pot on the stove or in the microwave in a heatproof bowl and heat until it just starts to simmer.

COOKIE

4 cups all-purpose flour

1 teaspoon baking soda

1 pound unsalted butter, room temperature

2½ cups packed brown sugar

1 cup granulated sugar

4 eggs

2 tablespoons vanilla extract

2 teaspoons salt

PEANUT BUTTER ICE CREAM

2 cups whole milk

2 cups cream

1¼ cups sugar

½ cup nonfat milk powder

1½ cups peanut butter

⅛ teaspoon xanthan gum

1 pinch salt

CONTINUED ➡

10. Whisk in the sugar, milk powder, peanut butter, xanthan gum, and salt. Use a hand blender to mix until smooth.

11. Chill in the fridge for 1 hour, then freeze for 30 minutes, until just below freezing.

12. Pour into an ice cream maker and freeze according to the manufacturer's instructions.

13. Return to the freezer until it becomes fairly solid but spreadable, another hour or so.

14. Repeat steps 9 through 12 for the jelly ice cream.

SANDWICH

15. Cut the cookie in half widthwise.

16. Spread the peanut butter ice cream evenly onto one of the cookie halves and freeze both cookie halves for 15 minutes.

17. Spread the jelly ice cream on top of the peanut butter ice cream. Press the other cookie half on top of the jelly ice cream. Freeze for at least 2 hours or overnight.

18. With a long, sharp, sturdy knife, slice the big sandwich into 3 × 3-inch cubes, then slice the cubes in half diagonally to create triangles.

19. Individually wrap and store in the freezer until ready to eat.

STRAWBERRY JELLY ICE CREAM

2 cups whole milk

2 cups cream

¼ cup sugar

1½ cups nonfat milk powder

1½ cups strawberry jelly

⅛ teaspoon xanthan gum

1 pinch salt

THE INGREDIENTS
OF A PB&J SANDWICH
COMBINED WITH ➡

THE INGREDIENTS OF
AN ICE CREAM SANDWICH
MAKE ➡

New Smash-in!
PB&J ICE CREAM
SANDWICH

BLUEBERRY PIE MILKSHAKE

MAKES	PREP TIME	COOK TIME	TOTAL TIME
8 to 10 milkshakes	1 hour 20 minutes	1 hour	2 hours 20 minutes

Is it really necessary to *make* a pie and then put it into the blender? Why not just blend the blueberries and some pie crust? Well, the cooked pie flavor adds so much to this milkshake. As you taste the bits of browned crust through the straw, you'll totally get it.

MAKE IT YOUR OWN➡ Any combo of pie and ice cream will work. Use your imagination. Cherry pie and chocolate ice cream, key lime pie and coconut ice cream, pecan pie and Oreo ice cream—you are the master of your own mash-up.

2 tablespoons softened butter, plus more for greasing

2 pie crusts, homemade or store bought

5 cups blueberries

1 cup sugar

3 tablespoons cornstarch

juice of 1 lemon

2 teaspoons vanilla extract

1 pinch salt

1 egg

2 tablespoons sugar

3 scoops vanilla ice cream per shake

1. Preheat the oven to 350°F.

2. Butter a pie pan and place the bottom crust inside.

3. In a bowl, mix the blueberries, sugar, cornstarch, lemon juice, vanilla, and salt and stir well to combine.

4. Pour the blueberry mixture into the crust.

5. Spread the softened butter evenly over the blueberry mixture.

6. Add the top pie crust and seal the edges. Score the top center of the pie with an X.

7. Whisk the egg with a splash of water. Brush the egg all over the top of the pie crust.

8. Sprinkle the sugar all over the top of the crust.

9. Bake until brown and bubbly, about 1 hour. You may need to add foil to the edges if they begin to burn before the rest of the pie cooks fully.

10. Remove from the oven and cool to room temperature.

11. Cut a slice of pie and add it to the blender with the ice cream. Blend until smooth.

12. Garnish the shake with a small chunk of pie.

PECAN PIE CANDY BAR

MAKES	PREP TIME	COOK TIME	TOTAL TIME
27 candy bars	3 hours	1 hour	4 hours

The filling of a pecan pie has that perfect nutty, caramel, nougaty texture that reminds me of a great candy bar, so I made candy bars from it. Making candy bars can prove a little tedious because you have to keep the chocolate at the right temperature and dip the bars one by one, but it's worth it and guaranteed to impress your friends and loved ones.

LITTLE PECAN GIFTS➡ To make these extra special, wrap the finished bars in decorative wax paper and tie them with ribbon. In winter, these should be fine at room temperature, but consider keeping them in the fridge for extra safekeeping.

butter for greasing

1 pie crust, homemade or store bought

2 cups pecan halves

9 tablespoons unsalted butter, melted

1½ cups packed brown sugar

½ cup honey

2 teaspoons vanilla extract

salt

3 eggs

1 pound chocolate chips

¼ cup heavy cream

1. Preheat the oven to 350°F.

2. Butter a 9 × 9-inch baking dish, line it with parchment paper, then butter the paper.

3. Roll out the pie crust so that it will cover the bottom of the dish and press it into the dish. It's OK if it comes up the sides a little.

4. Chop the pecans into smaller pieces.

5. Mix 6 tablespoons of the melted butter with the sugar, honey, vanilla, 2 pinches of salt, and eggs and whisk until uniform.

6. Add the pecans and combine.

7. Pour the pecan mixture into the baking dish.

8. Bake for 50 to 60 minutes, until it sets. Remove from the oven and refrigerate for 2 hours or overnight

9. Mix the chocolate, cream, and remaining 3 tablespoons of melted butter in a double boiler and gently heat, stirring often, until it melts. Be careful: overheating will cause it to seize. Stir in 1 pinch of salt.

10. Remove the pecan mixture from the pan and cut it into 27 (1 × 3-inch) rectangles. Depending on how uniform your pie looks and how pretty you want the final product to be, you may want to cut off the edges and make fewer bars.

THE INGREDIENTS
OF **PECAN PIE**
COMBINED WITH

↓

THE INGREDIENTS
OF A **CANDY BAR**
MAKE

↓

New
Smash-in!

PECAN PIE
CANDY BAR

11. One by one, dip the bars into the chocolate. Lift each out with two forks, allowing excess chocolate to drip back into the bowl. Allow the bars to cool on a piece of wax paper.

12. Keeping them on the paper, transfer the bars to the fridge to cool and fully harden.

HORCHATA & MEXICAN CHOCOLATE DACQUOISE

MAKES	PREP TIME	COOK TIME	TOTAL TIME
1 dacquoise, 12 to 24 servings	30 minutes	6 hours	6 hours 30 minutes

One of my roommates worked at Flour Bakery + Café in Boston, and she brought home some leftovers of a dacquoise. Being the bad roommate that I am, I stole some, and I'm so glad I did because it's not something I normally would order and I absolutely loved it. It has everything you want in a dessert. I had to figure out how to make it, and thankfully the owner, Joanne Chang, had posted the recipe. It's a beast and takes a long time, but if you bring this to a holiday party, your friends or family will go nuts. Mine did. That's the good news. The bad news is that you might have to start making it every year. I adapted this recipe from Joanne Chang's recipe for hazelnut-almond dacquoise.

MERINGUE

1. Preheat the oven to 225°F. Line a half sheet pan with parchment paper and with a pencil draw 3 (10 × 3-inch) rectangles on the paper, all a few inches apart from one another. Flip the paper over and grease it.

2. In a food processor, process the almonds to a powder but stop before they become a paste. Remove to a bowl.

3. Process the cereal to a powder and add it to the almonds.

4. Stir in the powdered sugar and salt.

5. In a stand mixer with the whip attachment, beat the egg whites on medium for 3 to 4 minutes, until they form soft peaks.

6. Add a third of the granulated sugar and mix for 30 seconds, until it incorporates. Repeat until all the sugar combines. Increase the speed to high and whip for 15 or so seconds. The meringue should look white and fairly stiff.

7. Sprinkle the cereal-nut mixture into the meringue and fold it in gently.

CONTINUED →

MERINGUE

butter for greasing

½ cup toasted almonds

1 cup puffed rice cereal, plus more for garnish

1 ⅓ cups powdered sugar

1 pinch salt

6 egg whites

⅓ cup granulated sugar

1 teaspoon cinnamon

GANACHE

1½ cups heavy cream

1 pound bittersweet chocolate chips

1 teaspoon cayenne powder

1 teaspoon cinnamon

COFFEE BUTTERCREAM

¾ cup sugar

2 eggs

1 egg yolk

¾ pound unsalted butter, room temperature, each cut into 2-inch chunks

2 single-serving packets instant coffee (expensive brand)

salt

8. Use a pastry bag or clean plastic storage bag with one corner snipped off to pipe the meringue into the rectangles on the baking sheet.

9. Bake for 3 hours, until the rectangles feel firm. Shut off the oven but leave the meringues in the oven for 3 more hours.

GANACHE

10. In the microwave, heat the cream on high for about 2 minutes, until steaming.

11. Place the chocolate in a bowl. Pour the hot cream into the chocolate and stir well until the chocolate melts. If it doesn't come together, microwave it on high for a few seconds.

12. Stir in the cayenne and cinnamon. This mixture should feel fairly hard at room temperature but soft when slightly warmer than room temperature (70°F). It's best to work with it when it's right on that line and firms up after you apply it.

BUTTERCREAM

13. In a small saucepan, stir together the sugar with ¼ cup of water. Bring to a boil and cook for about 4 minutes, until it reaches 238°F as measured on a candy thermometer.

14. In a stand mixer with the whip attachment, beat the eggs and yolk together for 3 minutes, until they look pale and light.

15. With the mixer on low, slowly drizzle the syrup into the eggs. Let it drip down the side of the bowl rather than hitting the whip attachment.

16. Increase the speed to medium and whip for 8 minutes. The mixture should look light, fluffy, and pale and feel cool.

17. Decrease the speed to low and add the butter, 4 chunks at a time. Increase the speed to medium and whip for 5 minutes.

18. Add the instant coffee and salt and whip on low for 1 minute or so, until combined. Plan to use the buttercream right away.

19. Carefully peel the meringues from the paper. Be careful because they're fragile, but It's not the end of the world if you break one.

20. Cut a 10 × 3-inch piece of cardboard (the same size as the meringue rectangles). Place 1 meringue on the cardboard, flat side down.

21. Cover the top of the meringue with a good layer of the softened ganache.

22. Place the second meringue, flat side up, on the ganache and gently press it in.

23. Spread a nice thick layer of the buttercream on top of the meringues.

24. Place the third meringue, flat side up, onto the buttercream. This will help make the top of the dacquoise flat.

25. Frost the cake with the remaining buttercream, making it as perfectly rectangular as you can.

26. Refrigerate for 1 hour so the buttercream becomes nice and solid.

27. Heat the ganache in 15-second intervals in the microwave on high until it's pourable and pour it over the cake. Aim for the chocolate to drip over and fully cover the entire cake. Try using a rack over wax or parchment paper so you can collect the excess chocolate to fill in the gaps. Doing it directly on a sheet of wax paper works, too.

28. Refrigerate right away so the chocolate hardens.

29. After 1 hour, the chocolate will have stiffened. Coat the sides of the cake with the puffed rice cereal, pressing the cereal into the side of the cake.

30. Refrigerate until ready to serve. Remove from fridge at least 1 hour before serving.

THE INGREDIENTS
OF HORCHATA
COMBINED WITH

THE INGREDIENTS
OF DACQUOISE
MAKE

New Mash-up!

HORCHATA & MEXICAN
CHOCOLATE DACQUOISE

FOUNDATION RECIPES

ALL-PURPOSE CURRY POWDER

1. In a dry frying pan, toast all ingredients except the turmeric on medium heat for about 5 minutes, watching carefully to prevent burning.

2. Grind the toasted spices in a spice grinder. Add turmeric after grinding.

1 tablespoon black mustard seed

1 tablespoon whole cardamom

1 tablespoon whole coriander

1 tablespoon whole cumin

1 tablespoon whole fenugreek

1 teaspoon black peppercorns

1 teaspoon whole allspice

1 teaspoon whole cloves

1 inch cinnamon bark

10 dried arbol chiles

2 teaspoons turmeric

CARNITAS

1. In a food processor, blend all ingredients except the pork.

2. Pour the mixture over the pork and marinate 8 hours or overnight.

3. Preheat the oven to 250°F.

4. Transfer the pork and marinade to an oven-safe pot. If needed, add a little water so the liquid reaches about a quarter of the way up the side of the pork.

5. Bake, uncovered, for about 6 hours, until the pork browns on the outside and is falling apart.

6. Shred with forks or your hands.

15 sprigs cilantro

2 shallots

6 cloves garlic

1 tablespoon chipotle powder

2 teaspoons black pepper

2 teaspoons cumin

1 pinch cinnamon

1 pinch ground cloves

2 teaspoons salt

2 cups orange juice

5 pounds pork shoulder (Boston butt), bone in

GARAM MASALA

1. In a dry frying pan, toast all ingredients on medium heat for about 5 minutes, watching carefully to prevent burning.

2. Grind them in a spice grinder.

2 tablespoons coriander seed

2 tablespoons cumin seed

2 tablespoons peppercorns

1 tablespoon deshelled cardamom

1 teaspoon whole cloves

3 inches cinnamon bark

1 bay leaf

GNOCCHI

1. Preheat the oven to 350°F.

2. Rub the potatoes with olive oil and season with salt and pepper.

3. Bake on a lined, oiled baking sheet for 90 minutes or until tender.

4. Remove from the oven and allow to cool for 15 minutes.

5. Remove the skins and run the potatoes through a food mill or potato ricer.

6. Mix the egg into the potatoes, add the flour, and mix until a dough forms. Add more flour as needed.

7. Roll the gnocchi dough into long ropes and cut into gnocchi-size pieces.

8. Roll each piece on the back of a fork to form the traditional gnocchi shape.

2 large russet potatoes

olive oil

salt and pepper

1 cup all-purpose flour

1 egg, beaten

MARINARA SAUCE

1. In a saucepan, heat the olive oil over medium heat.

2. Add the garlic and onion and cook for 2 minutes.

3. Add the tomatoes, oregano, salt, and pepper and simmer for 10 minutes.

¼ cup olive oil

2 cloves garlic, minced

2 tablespoons minced onion

1 (28-ounce) can crushed tomatoes

1 teaspoon dried oregano

salt and pepper

NAAN

1. With a cast iron pan inside, preheat the oven to 500°F.

2. Dissolve the yeast into 1 cup of warm water and let sit 10 minutes.

3. When the yeast looks frothy, add the yogurt, honey, flour, and salt and mix.

4. Transfer the dough to a floured surface and knead for 7 to 8 minutes. Add additional flour if needed.

5. Form the dough into a ball and coat with ghee. Let sit in a ghee-greased bowl for 1 hour, until the ball doubles in size.

6. Knead in the minced garlic and divide into 6 smaller balls.

7. Coat each ball in ghee and let sit for 30 minutes.

8. Roll each ball out into a flat disk and cover in ghee again.

9. Slap a dough disk onto the cast iron skillet. Flip after 1 minute, or when bubbles form.

10. Cook for about 1 more minute and remove from the oven to a plate lined with a kitchen towel. Repeat with the remaining dough.

1 packet active yeast

¼ cup yogurt

1 tablespoon honey

3 ½ cups all-purpose flour, plus more for dusting

1 teaspoon salt

clarified butter (ghee) for coating and greasing

2 cloves garlic, minced

PICO DE GALLO

1. Mix all ingredients and refrigerate until ready to use.

5 vine-ripened tomatoes, diced

1 red onion, diced

20 cilantro sprigs, finely chopped

3 to 5 jalapeño peppers, seeds removed and diced

1 clove garlic, grated

juice of 2 limes

1 teaspoon salt

PIZZA DOUGH

1. Mix 2½ cups of the flour with 1½ cups of cold water, the yeast, and the salt. Stir well with a wooden spoon for about 3 minutes. Refrigerate for 30 minutes.

2. By hand or in a stand mixer with the dough hook, stir the dough mixture for about 5 minutes. Slowly mix in the rest of the flour, ½ cup at a time. When you can no longer stir it by hand, pour it on to a floured surface and knead the dough for about 15 minutes, until smooth. (If using a stand mixer, continue to knead.)

3. Refrigerate the dough for 8 hours or overnight. Remove from the fridge 1 hour before using.

5 cups cold bread flour, plus more for dusting

1 tablespoon instant yeast

1 tablespoon salt

COMBO CHARTS

There's no single formula for mashing recipes together, but following the pattern outlined at the beginning of the book (pages x–xiii) makes it easier to create your own original recipes. Let's review.

To put you in the right frame of mind, here are some more sample charts that explain how I created additional recipes in the book.

STEP 1
Define the ingredients needed for each separate dish.

STEP 2
Pair down each list to the essentials while looking for common ingredients.

STEP 3
Build it back up.

STROGANOFF BURGER

STROGRANOFF		BURGER
noodles	→	bun
beef	→	burger
mushrooms	→	mushrooms
sour cream	→	topping
Cognac		

LOBSTER ROLL

LOBSTER ROLL BANH MI

BANH MI

lobster	➜	**lobster**	⬅ meat (pâté / headcheese)
mayonnaise	➜	**coconut, fish sauce, mint**	⬅ fish sauce
buttered toasted roll	➜	**toasted baguette**	⬅ baguette
		pickled carrot and radish	⬅ pickled carrot and radish
		cilantro	⬅ cilantro
		cucumber	⬅ cucumber
		jalapeño	⬅ jalapeño

MAC & CHEESE	HOT CRAB DIP	CRAB RANGOON MAC & CHEESE	CRAB RANGOON
pasta ➡	➡	pasta	
cheese ➡	cheese ➡	cheese	⬅ cheese
butter ➡	cream cheese ➡	cream cheese	⬅ cream cheese
	mayo	soy sauce	⬅ soy sauce
	crab ➡	crab	⬅ crab
milk ➡	➡	milk	
	scallions ➡	scallions	
	heat ➡	pickled jalapeños	
	paprika ➡	paprika	
		wonton wrappers	⬅ wonton wrappers

RICE & BEANS

rice

beans

spices

meat

tomatoes

TART

→ crust

→ filling

topping

DEVILED EGGS

eggs

mayo

mustard

paprika

chives

MAC & CHEESE DEVILED EGGS

pasta

→ eggs

cheese

milk

butter

→ mustard

→ paprika

→ chives

bacon (bonus!)

MAC & CHEESE

← pasta

← cheese

← milk

← butter

Here are some suggestions and blank tables for you to plan to execute your own mash-ups. Go crazy!

You can mash-up anything, but these foods have lots of mash-up potential:

---

burgers	eggs benedict	mac & cheese	stuffed mushrooms
burritos	french toast	nachos / totchos	stuffings
chicken & waffles	gnocchi	pasta / ravioli	tacos
chicken wings	jalapeño poppers	sandwiches	tamales
deviled eggs	lasagna	skewers / kabobs	
dips	loaded french fries	soups	

YOUR FAVORITE COMFORT FOODS

POTENTIAL MASH-UP MATCH

_____

_____

_____

_____

_____

_____

_____

THING #1   NEW THING!   THING #2

BURGER SMASH-IN

Anything you can hold in your hand without too much mess can function as a bun or sandwich bread. Here are my faves.

arepas
avocado
baklava
cinnamon
congealed noodles
cornbread
egg rolls
fried chicken
fried tofu
fritters
garlic bread
graham crackers
grilled cheese sandwich
hush puppies
large ravioli
latkes
mozzarella sticks
pancakes
pastry
pita
pizzas
portobello mushrooms
potato skins
quesadillas
scallion pancakes
soft pretzels
spring rolls
summer rolls
sushi rice
tater tots
tostones
waffles

FOOD TO TURN INTO A BURGER		BURGER
	→	bun
	→	burger
	→	
	→	topping(s)
	→	
	→	
	→	

If a certain fast-food chain has taught us anything, it's that anything can serve as a taco shell, including:

bacon weave	fried eggs	pancakes
Canadian bacon	fried lasagna	quesadillas
chicken cutlets	grilled cheese sandwiches	thin pizza
fried cheese	lettuce	

FOOD TO TURN INTO A TACO		TACO
	➡	shell
	➡	taco
	➡	meat
	➡	cheese
	➡	salsa
	➡	sour cream
	➡	lettuce

ACKNOWLEDGMENTS

Thank you to Sally for putting the team together and making everything happen to make this book possible. Thanks to Brian and Krissy for really going above and beyond at the photo shoots and to Aaron for making the vision come alive on the page and rolling with all the punches.

Thank you to James and everyone at Sterling for not only believing in my ability to write this book but also for managing the photography and design aspects so it really could be the book I wanted it to be.

Thank you to my family for the constant support, for showing up to events and episode tapings, and for not being skeptical about my career path (at least publicly). Thank you, Al, for bringing attention to The Food in My Beard across the country and now abroad and, Jo, for helping me stay hip—or at least appearing to be. And thank you Casey for publicly yelling at anyone who disagrees with my approach on social media.

Thanks to Georgina for being my number one publicist, diligently taste-testing all of my recipes, pushing me to reach new levels, and allowing our home to be an office, studio, and workshop for all of my crazy projects (many of which aren't even food related and often smell bad).

And to anyone who has followed me on any platform, watched a video, written a comment, or even pressed the "like" button one single time in the history of my blog. It's because of you that I am able to do what I do, and I feel grateful for that every single day. Even the guy who commented that he hopes that I fall into a fire the next time I roast a marshmallow.

INDEX